Randolph Crump Miller

Dr. Miller is Professor of Christian Education at the Yale Divinity School, Yale University where he has been since 1952. Before that he taught Religion, Theology and Christian Education at Church Divinity School of the Pacific, Berkeley, California. He is the author of a number of outstanding books in the field and is the editor of *Religious Education,* a bi-monthly journal of the Religious Education Association. For several years he has served as a consultant to the Division of Curriculum Development of the Protestant Episcopal Church.

CHRISTIAN
NURTURE
AND
THE
CHURCH

RANDOLPH CRUMP MILLER

CHRISTIAN
NURTURE
AND
THE
CHURCH

CHARLES SCRIBNER'S SONS
New York

To Frank who helped

PREFACE

This book is an exploration of the significance of the nature of the Church for Christian education. I have examined the Biblical and historical evidence for a doctrine of the Church, interpreted Christian education in the light of these findings, and applied the results to the life of the local congregation. Incidentally, this involves an evaluation of religious instruction in schools and Christian nurture in homes.

The basic theme is that the Church is the people of God and the body of Christ, a community in which the Holy Spirit is at work. It is a fellowship in which all baptized people share a ministry of love and reconciliation. It has an ordained ministry of those set apart for special functions, including preaching and the administration of the sacraments and leadership of the congregation. It is an exclusive body of those who have been called out, and yet it is world-wide in its scope and universal in its concern for all mankind.

The local congregation is the Church in a particular place; its educational aim is primarily to educate people to *be* the Church. This needs to be elaborated in terms of all the local parish's functions, relationships to the denomination, to the world-wide Church, and to the world.

Schools are valuable for providing education *about* religion, and this *should* be part of their cultural function, but schools cannot educate people to be the Church, except to the degree that a particular school or a specific classroom experience becomes a community of the Holy Spirit. Therefore, the local parish must have its own unique educational program to which the functions of the school are supplementary.

Education is not limited to instruction. In this book, I have used *instruction* as a description of the transmission of factual information and its interpretation; I have used *nurture* as a broader term to describe the involvement of the pupil in the atmosphere and relationships of a community, including knowledge about it as a means toward loyalty to it. Christian education is the nurture of the total person in all the relationships of life seen from the perspective of membership in the Christian community. This is a program "from womb to tomb."

The Christian family performs this function on an impermanent basis while children are in the home, but only the Church can do it for children or adults on a permanent basis. A close

relationship between parents and the parish is essential if the
family and Church are to cooperate in the major project of in-
corporating members into the body of Christ.

This book is a sequel to my previous ones, *The Clue to Christian Education* and *Biblical Theology and Christian Education*,
but it develops more fully the implications of those books in
terms of the understanding of the Church. The first formation of
the thesis was in connection with a series of lectures at the Eden
Theological Seminary and these lectures were revised and given
to groups of teachers during the past several years. In the present
form, I used these chapters as the basis for a series of lectures at
St. Augustine's College, Canterbury, England. In the meantime,
Howard Grimes wrote *The Church Redemptive* (Abingdon Press)
and approached the problem from very much the same point
of view.

During my sabbatical leave from Yale University, in 1959-1960,
I had the opportunity to be in residence at the Ecumenical Institute at Bossey, Switzerland, where the problem of the ministry
was discussed during a six-weeks period. After that I discussed
the theme of the book with educators in Germany, the Nether-
lands, Belgium, France, and England. I had access to St. Deiniol's
Library, Hawarden, in Wales, where I was in residence for a
period of uninterrupted writing. The visits to schools in Germany
and England convinced me that schools can provide religious instruction, but that they can never be a substitute for the Christian
nurture of the local congregation.

When I had completed this manuscript, I wrote a study guide
entitled *The Educational Mission of the Church* for the World
Council of Christian Education and Sunday School Association,
and in developing the same thesis I used some passages from this
book.

A grant from the American Association of Theological Schools
was of great assistance. Mr. William L. Savage of Charles Scribner's Sons was aware of the project from the beginning. My wife
has helped by reading and correcting the manuscript, as well as
by participating in endless discussions of the basic theme.

I have used translations of the Bible marked as follows:

> RSV—*Revised Standard Version* (copyright 1946, 1952, by the Divi-
> sion of Christian Education of the National Council of the
> Churches of Christ in the United States of America)

G—*The Complete Bible: An American Translation,* by J. M. Powis Smith and Edgar J. Goodspeed (copyright 1939 by the University of Chicago Press)

P—*The New Testament in Modern English,* by J. B. Phillips (copyright 1958 by J. B. Phillips, the Macmillan Co.).

I am indebted to these and other publishers in cases where they have granted me permission to quote copyrighted material.

RANDOLPH CRUMP MILLER

Yale University
The Divinity School

TABLE OF CONTENTS

CHRISTIAN
NURTURE
AND
THE
CHURCH

Part I

CHAPTER I

The Nature of the Church

How can Christian education be effective in a community which is not fully Christian? If education is what happens to a person in community, Christian education is what happens to a person within a Christian community. When one grows up within the life of a group, he takes on the coloration of the group. This is what occurs in home, school, church, and community. Each of these four institutions provides an environment in which growth toward specific goals takes place, and each one has depths of influence beyond what one sees on the surface. But there is also an overarching influence of our culture which permeates all of our smaller groupings.

Today's society is primarily a secular one, although there may be varying degrees of Christian influence at certain levels of its social, industrial, and political life. We may still talk of Western Christendom, but an analysis of the motives by which the individuals, groups, and nations of the West behave casts doubts on any assumption that they are primarily Christian. We have a residue of Christian ethics which is inherent in our laws and customs, but there is little sense of the joyousness and integrity of Christian faith remaining.

The Church lives in this modern world, and it is not in a position to have a direct effect on the assumptions of contemporary culture even though its message is to the world. But we as Christians are capable of dealing with the Church as we find it, especially in the local congregation. If we can come to an understanding of the nature of the Church, beginning with the picture drawn in the New Testament, and then seek by God's grace to

1

reproduce the essence of the Church's nature in the local congregation, we can provide a community in which a Christian educational influence will prevail.

This can be illustrated in a negative way by observing the fruits of religious instruction in secular schools. In England and West Germany are two of the best systems in the world for providing religious instruction in state schools. The teachers are well-trained, the syllabi are carefully developed, and the classes are compulsory unless the parents request that their children not participate. Worship is part of the program. There can be no doubt that the younger generation is provided with religious information. They are better informed than young Christians in any other country. But there is a universal report that there is practically no transfer to Church loyalty. In West Germany, according to information from Church youth leaders, the children are confirmed at fourteen years of age, and this is the occasion for social celebrations. Most of them leave school at the same age and usually begin work. But only a minority of them are found in Church-sponsored meetings or at worship. Somewhere along the way, in spite of lengthy confirmation instruction from their pastors, their intellectual grasp of Biblical information has failed to make any connection with the Christian community.

Some leaders believe that this is due to overemphasis on the intellectual side. When this occurs, Christianity is reduced to a system of concepts which may or may not challenge the mind, and this leads to a disastrous misinterpretation of the claim of the Christian faith on one's life. *Religious instruction is not to be equated with Christian nurture.*

If Scripture is taught effectively, so that it begins to capture the total personality of the pupil, a supporting community for his beliefs cannot be found in a school based on secular presuppositions. The school curriculum, derived primarily from a Greek view of life, is not consistent with the Jewish-Christian interpretation of God at work through his people in history. Therefore, the Christian attitudes are likely to be overwhelmed because there is no support for them. This dissolving of religious convictions often leaves a permanent scar.

In these same countries, as in the United States, there are many private and parochial schools in which religious instruction is given. But the results are not startlingly different because every school places the emphasis on instruction and inculcates the values of the surrounding culture. What is lost sight of is the affection and personal relationships which need to stand at the center of any community in which religion may be taught effectively.[1]

Unless religious instruction is supported by a community which lives by the truths taught, it may be both useless and dangerous. When the Church and home are to some degree communities of the Holy Spirit in which the pupil feels he belongs, the information provided by the schools becomes a means for his Christian nurture. The crucial point is not the secularism of our school systems, which represent the culture in which we live, but the genuine Christian community life of the local congregation and the homes which are attached to it.

Religious instruction in state schools is possible in many countries and it obviously has great value in assisting the pupil in understanding his heritage. He cannot get a well-rounded view of history or literature without dealing with religion. He cannot understand the democratic assumptions of the American way of life without being acquainted with the Christian elements in the Bill of Rights or the Constitution. He cannot understand the religious elements in the culture of the West without a grasp of the Jewish-Christian history contained in the Scriptures. These are purely secular reasons for objective religious instruction, and they provide a basis for such instruction even in countries where there is separation of Church and state.

Beyond this, religious instruction can have three additional values. First, because every school is not exclusively secular and some schools are founded in Christian principles, the sense of community will to some degree reinforce the information about religion, and the school to this extent will do the job of the Church. Second, the Christian witness of the teacher breaks through in any environment and especially in a favorable one, and therefore no school hiring Christian teachers can avoid this possibility. Third, the information provided by the school, when favorably received, becomes a basis for the Church's educational task.

The Church is primarily concerned with *education to be the*

---

[1] See Kenneth E. Hyde, *The Communication of Ideas and Attitudes Among Secondary School Children* (University of Birmingham, 1959), unpublished Ph.D. dissertation.

Church. By this, I mean that Christians become such within the Christian community. The crucial factor is not information as such, not the capturing of the mind, not the passing of an examination. The significant factor in Christian education is helping the individual, by God's grace, to become a believing and committed member of the community of the Holy Spirit, obedient to Christ as his Lord and Master, and living as a Christian to the best of his ability in all his relationships. This involves the whole work of the Church, not just classes for various age levels. It is a nurturing process in the broadest sense, for the total personality of the individual in all his relationships is involved. He is being formed as a person by all kinds of influences, and the Church's task is to lead him to the point where he can make a commitment on his own and maintain it in the face of all the obstacles which life may place before him.

What happens depends on the Church's view of itself, and this forces us back to the problem of the nature of the Church. If we are to educate people to be the Church, we need to see clearly how the Church of Jesus Christ is realized in the life of the local congregation. This is the inescapable problem we must face before we can analyze the crisis in Christian education in our time. The nature of the Church, its ministry, its teaching, its reality in the local congregation, and its relation to the world are involved in such an analysis. Then we can continue by examining the functions of the local congregation and their significance for Christian education.

THE CHURCH IN THE BIBLE

We can discover a picture of the Church in the New Testament, a picture which becomes more meaningful when we already know the Old Testament background. But those who seek a definition which is precise and comprehensive must find the New Testament imagery very frustrating. For, says Paul Minear, "the very nature of these idioms makes a set of precise conclusions impossible. But even though such a study leads us farther and farther from the goal of an accurate and exact doctrine, this in itself may yield greater comprehension of the magnitude of the Christian community. The reality may be of such a nature that the more we understand it, the less we are able to draw its boundaries and mark its terrain. Does this mean, then, that the efforts to relate the Una Sancta to the church in Grover's Corners must be given up as an impossible task? Must we forsake the empirical church for the heavenly church? Not at all. For all of the New Testament efforts to describe the scope and scale of the church's life presuppose one thing. They presuppose that we are in close and intimate communion with a congregation. It is life together which enables us to comprehend the glory of God. And this life together is possible only in some town, whether it be Grover's Corners or Grundy Center."[2]

This richness of New Testament imagery is overwhelming. The Church is those "called by my name." "my mother and my brothers," "the Israel of God." It is "the temple of the Lord." It is to be "one flock, one shepherd." It is those who "acknowledge" or "confess" that Jesus is the Christ. It is the "called, chosen, sent" or "elect." It is a family in which one helps his "brothers and sisters."[3]

Certain terms stand out with particular relevance for our time. They describe the Church in organic ways, showing the interrelatedness of the members among themselves and with the God of Jesus Christ. It is not an individual matter, "for where two or three are gathered in my name, there am I in the midst of them" (Matt. 18:20, RSV). For our purposes, we need to look at such Biblical concepts as new covenant, people of God, those who are called out, the body of Christ, the community of the Holy Spirit, and followers of the way.

The Biblical story recounts the mighty acts of God, who appears as creator, as covenant giver, in Christ, in the Church, and at the consummation. We enter this Biblical drama through the Church, and therefore the history of God's people becomes our history. In Christ we find reconciliation with God and man, and the Church is the result of Christ's impact on history. The Old Covenant with Israel is superceded or completed by the New Covenant with God in Christ Jesus.[4]

[2] Paul S. Minear, *Horizons of Christian Community* (St. Louis: Bethany Press, 1959), p. 102.

[3] See Paul S. Minear, *Images of the Church in the New Testament* (Philadelphia: Westminster Press, 1960), pp. 268-69, for a list of 96 images. Of these, 27 are mentioned in the following pages. See also, Paul S. Minear, *Jesus and His People* (New York: Association Press, 1956), pp. 92-93, for a convenient summary of 24 such images.

[4] See below, pp. 38-43; also my *Biblical Theology and Christian Education* (New York: Charles Scribner's Sons, 1956), for a fuller treatment of this point of view.

NEW COVENANT

At the Last Supper, Jesus said, "This is my blood of the covenant, which is poured out for many" (Mark 14:24, RSV). Thus the concept of the covenant was continued from Israel's history. The distinctive note of the covenant was that Yahweh had chosen Israel. He had taken an insignificant race of slaves and led them out of Egypt. He had made them into a nation. They were expected to keep their part of the agreement; but whether they did or not, God would be faithful. Out of this gracious act of God came the ethical insights of the Hebrew prophets, with their insistence that Yahweh was just, righteous, and loving, their distrust of empty ceremonial, and their faith that God was Lord of history and would redeem Israel.

This was the Church of the Old Testament, founded on a covenant, based on a brotherhood which remembered the past and knew God's mighty acts in the present, living according to a holy Book, and open to foreigners. It had certain marks, such as circumcision, based on the Law. This was the community to which Jesus belonged, "as a loyal layman and son of the covenant. . . . He never repudiated his membership."[5]

This sense of continuity between the old and the new covenant is evident in the New Testament writings. Abraham, says Paul, is "the father of us all" (Romans 4:16, RSV). The first mission of the Christian community was to Jews, and Christianity was considered a Jewish sect, continuing to worship in the temple (Acts 2:46; 3:1).

This continuity with Israel was a basic factor in early Christianity. The covenant had been renewed, but they were still the Israel of God. They did not separate from Israel, but in time the Jews cast them out. But there was a difference. Even though the old and new Israel shared the same Bible, those of the new covenant read the Bible with a different perspective. Nationalism vanished under Paul. The presence of the Holy Spirit freed the primitive Church from the traditions of the old Israel and often offended those of the established faith. But this was not enough to make more than a new sect. The major distinction between the old and the new was in the covenant of Jesus' death and resurrection. The Christ had come and was Lord of the new community.

[5] Sherman E. Johnson, *The Nature of the Church in the Light of Scripture* (Cambridge, Mass.: Episcopal Evangelical Fellowship, 1944), p. 8.

The Messiah so long promised had come. This Jesus of Nazareth, known in the flesh by many people, had died and risen again, and now he was known as the living Lord of a living community. The chief actor in this formation of a new covenant was the God of Abraham, Isaac, and Jacob, but in Christ he had done "a new thing" and the result was a new community.

In Christ, God acted to form a new agreement with his people, and this is our inheritance through the ages. The Church today, with all its tortuous history, is still the people of the new covenant. The story of Israel is its story; the God revealed as the giver of the covenant is its God. God is faithful to his agreement, which Jeremiah described: "I will make a new covenant with the house of Israel. . . . I will put my law within them. . . . I will be their God, and they shall be my people. . . . I will forgive their iniquity, and I will remember their sin no more" (Jeremiah 31:31,33,34, RSV). The fulfillment of the covenant is found in the life, death, and resurrection of Jesus Christ. "This cup," said Jesus, "is the new covenant in my blood. Do this, as often as you drink it, in remembrance of me." (I Corinthians 11:25, RSV).

PEOPLE OF GOD

"But you are a chosen race, a royal priesthood, a holy nation, God's own people, that you may declare the wonderful deeds of him who called you out of darkness into his marvelous light" (I Peter 2:9, RSV). The Lord promised that he would dwell among the people of Israel (Exodus 29:45), and this idea was transformed in the New Testament. "The Israel of God" (Galatians 6:16) had become God's people because of what God had done for them through Jesus Christ.

One belonged to the "household of faith" (Galatians 6:10) as an individual, and yet the corporateness of the Church was plainly to be seen. One inherited his membership in a race or nation, and yet he exerted his citizenship. He was born into a household, and yet he knew himself as a family member. The group was primary, and the individual's significance was derived from the community and from Jesus Christ, its Head. "Here there cannot be Greek and Jew, circumcised and uncircumcised, barbarian, Scythian, slave, free man, but Christ is all, and in all" (Colossians 3:11, RSV).

This membership in the Church was not automatic. "Once

you were no people but now you are God's people; once you had not received mercy but now you have received mercy" (I Peter 2:10, RSV). Before we become God's people we live in darkness and do not experience mercy. God brings his people into being through his mercy, and in response his people declare his wonderful deeds. The Church is a reality of history, the product of the living God who has established a new relationship with his people. "I will be a father to you, and you shall be my sons and daughters" (II Corinthians 6:18, RSV). We do not understand how this happens, but we do experience the fact that it does happen. God takes a people, his good news is proclaimed, and the Holy Spirit is received by repenting men.

When the Church is seen as the people of God, there are certain important consequences. First, the Church has a sense of history. This history goes back to creation and to the selection of Israel as a chosen people. The God of Abraham is the Father of Jesus Christ. But it also means that the Church has a history from Pentecost, and its total nature includes this period of development. Second, the Church's solidarity depends on God, and therefore it does not depend on the goodness of its members. "It is the group that sanctifies, not vice versa," wrote Burton Scott Easton,[6] and this means that we are made whole as individuals because we are in the Church, but it also opens up the question of the quality of life in the local congregation. Third, this membership includes the absolute demand of a loving God, the result of which is a sense of ethical responsibility and of concern for one's neighbor, both in terms of interpersonal relationships and in terms of social and political responsibility. The people of God are "heirs of God and fellow heirs with Christ" (Romans 8:17, RSV).

EKKLESIA

Paul wrote to "the church of God which is at Corinth" (I Corinthians 1:2). The word translated church, *ekklesia,* has both secular and sacred meanings, being simply an assembly or a congregation, or those who are "called out." It is used in the New Testament in many different ways, sometimes referring to a single community, sometimes to the whole Church, and some-

[6] B. S. Easton, *Early Christianity*, ed. by Frederick C. Grant (Greenwich: Seabury Press, 1954), p. 121.

times to churches in the plural.[7] The question is whether the starting point in the thought of primitive Christianity was the Church as a whole or the local congregations. When "Aquila and Priscilla, together with the church in their house, send you hearty greetings in the Lord" (I Corinthians 16:19, RSV), it is obvious that this refers to a small local group, just as the references to "the churches of Asia" refer to plural congregations. There is the same confusion here as in present-day usage, when we go to *a* church and belong to *the* Church and believe the "holy Catholic Church."

There is a tension between two ideas in *ekklesia:* it is a congregation of persons and it is a group the members of which have been called out by God. The Church is a human community, with all the limitations that this suggests, and yet it shares "in a heavenly call" and has Jesus as "the apostle and high priest of" its "confession" (Hebrews 3:1, RSV). It is primarily spiritual in that the emphasis is on the love of God and the leading of the Holy Spirit, but it is not formless. It has various ministries and it has two sacraments, but the emphasis is on the divine power coming from the Father through the Spirit.

Emil Brunner builds his concept of the Church on the meaning of *ekklesia*, insisting on what seems to me to be a partial but significant truth. He writes that the *ekklesia* "is a pure communion of persons and has nothing of the character of an institution about it."[8] Everything else is secondary, especially the Lord's Supper and the institutional structure of the Church. Finally, he says, the members come to the place at which they "now *receive* the Body of Christ, instead of *being* the Body of Christ."[9] This leads to an exaltation of the priest as the dispenser of grace and to a view of the laity as passive recipients.

There are views of the Church current today which justify Brunner's criticism, but the answer does not lie in what Theodore Wedel calls "ecclesiastical primitivism."[10] It is true that the New Testament Church had a sense of community which is lack-

---

[7] See Johannes Weiss, *Earliest Christianity* (New York: Harper & Bros., 1959), II, 615, for a convenient summary of Biblical references, and pp. 615-622 for an interpretation.

[8] *The Misunderstanding of the Church* (Philadelphia: Westminster Press, 1953), p. 17.

[9] *Ibid.*, p. 77.

[10] *The Coming Great Church* (New York: Macmillan & Co., 1946), p. 7.

ing in the modern Church, but it is equally evident that the early Church had a structure. It was this structure that gave it a permanent basis and enabled it to survive, and it was the gathering of the *ekklesia* for worship, including the Lord's Supper, which provided the inward power. As Wedel writes, "Christians need each other, and they need the communal home of an institutional Church. They need the witness of historic tradition; they need outward and visible sacraments. They need an ecumenical Church order."[11]

Both Brunner and Wedel are insisting on essentials of Church life. The roots of both emphases are found in the New Testament community, and the problem is to find the right balance. And the balance is on the side of the community of persons. Unless the Holy Spirit is present in the interpersonal relations of the believers, the Church will become static, but enthusiasm and love may evaporate without ritual and organization. Paul's view of the Church subordinated the institutional, but he was never oblivious to it. When Paul talked about various ministries, he spoke within a wider context of faith in Jesus Christ or the call of God to all men. He offered no specific details about either the ministry or the celebration of a sacrament. Baptism Paul took for granted because it was already a universally accepted practice: "You were washed, you were sanctified, you were justified in the name of the Lord Jesus Christ and in the Spirit of our God" (I Corinthians 6:11, RSV). Repentance and faith were prior to baptism, and God acted to wash away one's sins; therefore, one was to be obedient. The moral and the sacramental go together. Paul also found the Lord's Supper as a tradition of the primitive community. It may have been combined with a fellowship meal at Corinth, but it also in some way permitted the community to remember and participate in Christ's death, and to anticipate his coming again. It was furthermore an act of unity: "Because there is one loaf, we who are many are one body, for we all partake of the same loaf" (I Corinthians 10:17, RSV).[12]

Brunner is right when he insists that the sacramental becomes dangerous when it is not based on personal fellowship in the

[11] *Ibid.*, p. 9.

[12] See George Johnston, *The Church in the New Testament* (Cambridge: at the University Press, 1943), pp. 95-99; Johannes Weiss, *Earliest Christianity*, II, 629-651.

community. Holy Communion has become a barrier to the unity of the Church. But, it seems to me, he is throwing away much that is essential to the meaning of *ekklesia*.

THE BODY OF CHRIST

"Now you are the body of Christ and individually members of it" (I Corinthians 12:27, RSV). This stresses the organic relationship between believers and the risen Lord. They are so intimately related to each other in Christ's body that they can no more be separated than can the members of a human body. "There is one body and one Spirit, just as you were called to the one hope that belongs to your call, one Lord, one faith, one baptism, one God and Father of us all, who is above all and through all and in all. But grace was given to each of us according to the measure of Christ's gift" (Ephesians 4:4-7, RSV). Here we see both organic unity and differentiation. The members do not have the same tasks, but they remain related.

The analogy of the body is particularly rich in its Christian associations. Paul did not use it in terms of accurate biological language, but as a representation of the unity of the members in Christ. It is closely related also to the idea of the broken body on the cross and to the body broken in the Holy Communion. Already there were divisions in the primitive Church, and the analogy of the "one body" was an appeal for Christian unity. Here were parties of the Church, there were the Judaizers, and everywhere were the petty disputers, and all of them threatened the unity of the fellowship in Christ.

In another direction, we are told that Christ is the head of the body. It is in this sense that the members are ruled by that member who governs. The integrity or wholeness of the body is derived from Christ.

Paul wrote that the members of the body are "in Christ," and this means that there has been a gift of a new relationship because of what God has done for us in Christ. "Therefore, if anyone is in Christ, he is a new creation" (II Corinthians 5:17, RSV). When we participate in Christ's new humanity, we recognize Christ's headship of the body. This is pictured in a different way when the Church is called the bride of Christ or when it is thought of as the vine and the branches.

Claude Welch writes that the fullness of individual personality is not lost. "The many are not swallowed up in the one, but remain many members." At the same time, "There is no purely private Christianity."[13] The Church is always an assembly of individuals, and yet it is always more than its members, because it is infused by the spirit of Christ as Lord.

If we remain attached to the figure of the body as the only analogy of the Church, there is the danger of misunderstanding and then the Church may be turned inward. Yet we know that the Church is in the world and has a mission to the world. If Christ is the head of the body, the members must represent him in the world. Not only is there the responsibility to draw all mankind into the body, but also there is the duty to share Christ's ministry to all mankind. This becomes the basis for both personal and social ethics. Christ's body yearns for all mankind, and we are the arms to do the reaching.

KOINONIA

At Pentecost, we are told that the newly baptized "devoted themselves to the apostles' teaching and fellowship, to the breaking of bread and the prayers" (Acts 2:42, RSV). The Elder writes in the hope that "you may have fellowship with us; and our fellowship is with the Father and with his Son Jesus Christ" (I John 1:3, RSV). Paul speaks of "participation in the Spirit" (Philippians 2:1, RSV) and of participation in the body and blood of Christ (I Corinthians 10:16). "God can be depended on, and it was he who called you to this fellowship with his Son, Jesus Christ our Lord" (I Corinthians 1:9, G). *Koinonia* means fellowship, participation, sharing, communion, community, and it is related to Christ, to the Father, and to the Holy Spirit.

The Church is a Christian community because its members participate in Christ and share the gifts of God. Because one is in fellowship with God, he is enabled to be in fellowship with his neighbors. Yet, this is almost too easy a distinction. One's fellowship with God *is* his fellowship with his neighbors, and one's fellowship with his neighbors *is* his fellowship with God. One cannot love God and hate his neighbor. The basic idea here is "participation in something in which others also participate,"[14]

---

[13] Claude Welch, *The Reality of the Church* (New York: Charles Scribner's Sons, 1958), pp. 167, 165; see all of chapter 5 on "The Body of Christ."

[14] J. Y. Campbell, "KOINONIA and Its Cognates in the New Testament," in *Journal of Biblical Literature*, LI, 353, quoted by J. R. Nelson, *The Realm of Redemption*, p. 53.

which is on a level deeper than fellowship or community in the modern sense. "The early Christian community," says John Knox, "was a sharing in a common memory and a common Spirit."[15]

The common memory became the apostles' teaching, which was based on their eye-witness accounts of what Jesus had said and done. The proclamation of what was remembered became the basis for preaching and worship, especially in the Lord's Supper. The good news was spread as people shared it with others by the power of the Spirit. The quality of life in the community was made possible because of the sharing of the Spirit, and this Spirit was identical with God's love at work in the interpersonal relations of those in the community. "The Spirit of the new community," writes Knox, "was no humanly generated comradeship; it was the very love of God poured out in Christ and uniting those who received it with one another because it united them also with him."[16]

The *koinonia* is something more than the fellowship generated in various clubs. It is deeper than what is found in a tea party. It is greater than team or school or company spirit. It is grounded in the Holy Spirit. It is found in the Church, in so far as the congregation is a Church, and yet it may be found outside the Church. There is a "secular work of the Holy Spirit" which is recognizable, and those in the Church who cannot see the evidence had better look again at their own fellowship. The insistence that the Church is primarily a *koinonia* of the Spirit is correct; it is the basis of the Church's unity in Christ, and of the unity of the members in the one body.

This outgoing of the Spirit into the world is what makes possible the missionary enterprise of the Church. Wherever, by the power of the Spirit, a member reaches out to another, the Church's mission is proclaimed. It may be what we call "foreign" missions, or it may be a helping hand to the neighbor next door; it may be in terms of prayer or in work for slum clearance; it may be an expression of concern for the reconciliation of a man and wife or for the program of planned parenthood.

Chiefly, the concept of *koinonia* helps us to remember that the Church is a fellowship of persons, given to men by the recon-

[15] John Knox, *The Early Church and the Coming Great Church* (Nashville: Abingdon Press, 1955), p. 52.
[16] *Ibid.*, p. 62; see pp. 50-62.

ciling love of God through the life, death and resurrection of Jesus Christ, and continuing through the power of the Holy Spirit. It is an experienced relationship, found in the life of the total Church generally and in the life of the specific congregation in particular. Therefore, it exists to some extent in every group called a Church, but no particular Church is identical with it.

THE WAY

The Church was called "the Way" (Acts 9:2) while Saul was still persecuting it. Later, this "Way" was called "a sect" by its opponents. (Acts 24:14). We read that Felix had "a rather accurate knowledge of the Way" (Acts 24:22, RSV), and that "there arose no little stir concerning the Way" (Acts 19:23, RSV) when the silversmiths lost business because people stopped buying silver idols. The Way was not a sect, it was *the* Way of life, made possible because of the resurrection of Jesus Christ. It was "a new and living way," but it was not primarily a road *to* anywhere; it was a manner of living. This is brought out most clearly in the Fourth Gospel when Jesus says, "I am the way" (John 14:6). The disciples did not know where Jesus was going, and in the end the answer was, "I am the way." The beginning and the end of the Way are the same thing, for as long as we are on the Way we have already come to the Father.

Evelyn Cummins has expressed this in her hymn:

> "I know not where the road will lead
>   I follow day by day,
> Or where it ends: I only know
>   I walk the King's highway. . . .
> The way is truth, the way is love,
>   For light and strength I pray,
> And through the years of life, to God,
>   I walk the King's highway. . . .
> Through light and dark the road leads on
>   Till dawns the endless day,
> When I shall know why in this life
>   I walk the King's highway."[17]

[17] Evelyn Atwater Cummins, in *The Hymnal 1940* (Church Pension Fund) No. 432. Used by permission of the author. Compare Paul Minear: "If we know the right road to choose, we do not need to know its end," in *Jesus and His People*, p. 38.

This way of love is what commended Christianity to the heathen. They could see that Christians loved one another, which was surprising enough, but they found that this love was outgoing and included the non-Christian. They saw in this loyalty to Christ the courage to stand in the face of opposition and of death. They observed the Christians' consistency in worship and action. Here was evident the ethical core of Christian living. The followers of the Way stirred up the silversmiths, they had themselves brought to trial, and yet their enemies could not give a reason for opposing or hating them.

The first Palestinian followers of Christ preferred this title of "the Way." It came out of the experience of the gift of the Holy Spirit at Pentecost, which made it possible for all men and women to be as intimately in Christ as were the Twelve. People were either in the Way or they were not, and as the community grew the question was forced on Jews first and then Gentiles. As Gentiles came into the believing fellowship, the Jewish members had to rethink their faith, and finally those in the Way became a united congregation in which the distinction between Jew and Gentile was lost. Those in the Way were assured of their salvation; they were good.

This emphasis on perfection could be maintained in the face of the expected coming of the kingdom, but the problem of what to do about sinners arose quickly. Toleration was suggested in II Timothy, but this practice did not last long, and the most generous view appeared in the *Shepherd of Hermas,* in which it was advocated that a person who sinned greatly could be forgiven only once.[18]

The Way was narrow in its demands for perfection and broad in its outreach to others. It became separated from Judaism as it became more surely centered in its foundation stone, Jesus Christ.

SIN IN THE CHURCH

The assumption that the followers of the Way were already saved was combined with the recognition of the continuance of sin. Although gross sin could lead to expulsion, Paul's approach to the sins of the members of the Corinthian congregation did not lead him to unchurch them. The reading of Church history

---

[18] See B. S. Easton, *Early Christianity,* pp. 127-134.

leads one to the belief that not only Church members but the Church as an organization may be guilty of every kind of disloyalty to Christ. Even though the members be redeemed, they remain sinners: this is the paradox which faces us at every level of Church life. Individuals, who by God's grace achieve a high degree of loyalty to Christ and thereby gain either the praise of good men or the condemnation of evil men, always fail at some point. The Church is always the *people* of God, and often the corporate acts of the Church, because they are social, are even less revealing of God's love than the acts of its members. Just as individuals need renewal and reform, so the Church has needed renewal and reform.

Much of what Paul said about the New Testament community needs to be understood against the historical background. The claims he made for the unity of the one body were against the background of actual divisions. Already there was the scandal of division, as some followed Peter and others Apollos and others Paul; and against this Paul claimed that they were united in Christ (I Corinthians 1:12-13). The controversy between Paul and the Judaizers almost led to a complete split into two groups (Galatians 2:11-14). The conclusion is obvious: "The united church of tomorrow cannot be modeled after the divided church of the first century," says John Knox.[19]

But at least the New Testament community sought to stay together. There was the shared life of the Spirit and the shared faith in Jesus Christ as Lord. The Church was an event of revelation; God had acted in history through Jesus Christ and the result was the Church as a new kind of human community. As the community became conscious of itself as the new covenant, the people of God, the *ekklesia,* the body of Christ, the *koinonia,* the followers of the Way, and many other designations, it was able to express what it potentially could be in Christ. The promise of God's mercy had been fulfilled in Christ and could be found in the Church. But the Church is always the people, and the people were never complete in their loyalty to the new covenant any more that the Israelites were complete in their loyalty to the old covenant. The redemptive love of God was at work in their midst and they had become the channels of God's

[19] John Knox, *op. cit.,* p. 16.

redemption, and yet their own reconciliation with God and men was never complete. The Church stands under judgment, and the kingdom has not fully come.

EDUCATION IN THE CHURCH

We have said that one becomes a Christian within a Christian community. Education takes place in community. This means that we need to take the idea of *koinonia* very seriously if we are to educate people to be the Church, for the people to be educated must be brought into that "atmosphere in which grace flourishes." The problem becomes clearer. Unless the local congregation becomes aware of what it means to be the Church, we cannot expect genuine Christian nurture to take place. But we must start with the Church as it is, much like the Corinthian Church with its divisions, its overt sinners, and its difficulties in discipline. If the Church of today is not like the ideal portrayed in the New Testament, neither was the Church of the New Testament like that picture. This may mean only that misery loves company and therefore that we can settle back into our usual ways; but it may mean that we will seek to become the Way. Only when we acknowledge our sin can we be ready for the forgiveness promised through the sacrificial love of God revealed in the cross. Only as we forgive those who trespass against us, can we expect God to forgive us our trespasses. This is what happens in the life of the congregation when it becomes aware of its condition as separated from God and of the promise of a renewed relationship with him. This is what the worship of the Church is all about, this is what the fellowship of the Church is for as the members become the means of God's reconciling love, this is what happens as the Church reaches out to those who do not know Christ, this is what occurs through pastoral care, this is what we proclaim and teach, and this is what we witness to in the unity that is promised anew as God works through the ecumenical movement.

The Church has a total ministry, which includes its educational responsibility; the Church has a body of belief to be communicated; the Church has a relationship to the world; the Church must come alive in the local congregation, for we find *the* church of Christ through our membership in *a* Church.

CHAPTER II

The Church's Ministry

WE HAVE said that the Church is the *people* of God. In both the Old and the New Testaments, the word for people is *laos,* from which come our words laity and lay person. In its original meaning, all members of the Church are the laity. The word has degenerated in its meaning so that for some it refers to second-class citizens, the privates in the Lord's army, who do not know very much about the faith. Even in the second century, as the clergy emerged out of the laity, a difference of status developed. But in the beginning the apostles and others shared in a ministry (*diakonia*).

Diakonia originally meant a waiter at table. This was the task of the earliest deacons in Acts, but it also included the idea of service or ministry in a much wider sense. There is here a reflection of Jesus' saying: "Whoever would be great among you must be your servant" (Mark 10:43, RSV). Christians are to serve each other in love. There may be many varieties of ministry, but these are differences of function and not of status. Even he who was the Messiah was also a servant. Christ's ministry was unique, but we participate in Christ's ministry by serving him, and this means serving each other in the Church and in the world.[1]

THE LAITY

"But you are a chosen race, a royal priesthood, a holy nation, God's own people" (I Peter 2:9 RSV). This priesthood of all believers, or priesthood of the laity, is evident throughout the New Testament. It includes both men and women, both ordained and unordained. Indeed, the place of women as fully part of the laity is an essential note of the New Testament Church. They functioned as teachers and prophets. John Knox suggests that

[1] See Hendrik Kraemer, *A Theology of the Laity* (Philadelphia: Westminster Press, 1958) p. 143.

18

Prisca was a prophet and teacher (Acts 18:26) and Phoebe was a deaconess or at least active in the ministry (Romans 16:1). The references to widows suggest that they not only were persons in need but also served as deaconesses.[2] The "royal priesthood" of I Peter is in the context the people of God and is really a description of the Church. If Jesus Christ is the high priest, then just as we are members of his body so we are members of his priesthood.

The laity take part in Christ's ministry of reconciliation. They are called to a variety of service, and the only differences are in terms of function. The Christian's witness to his faith in Christ takes place both within and outside the Church. He goes from the Church to the world and carries his commitment to God into his work and play. Because he is saved by grace through faith, therefore he is to be worthy of his calling (Ephesians 4:1). Men are called to different tasks, but for the same purpose: "for the equipment of the saints, for the work of ministry, for building up the body of Christ" (Ephesians 4:12, RSV).

The Second Assembly of the World Council of Churches, held at Evanston in 1954, reported that "in daily living and work the laity are not mere fragments of the church who are scattered about in the world and who come together again for worship, instruction and specifically Christian fellowship on Sundays. They are the church's representatives, no matter where they are. It is the laity who draw together work and worship; it is they who bridge the gulf between the church and the world, and it is they who manifest in word and action the Lordship of Christ over the world which claims so much of their time and energy and labour. This, and not some new order or organization, is the ministry of the laity. They are called to it because they belong to the church, although many do not yet know that they are thus called."[3]

APOSTLESHIP

There are two starting points for understanding the Church's ministry: one is the idea of the *laos*, the ministry of the whole

[2] See John Knox, "The Ministry in the Primitive Church," in *The Ministry in Historical Perspectives*, ed. by H. Richard Niebuhr and Daniel Day Williams (New York: Harper & Bros., 1956), pp. 16-17.

[3] W. A. Visser 't Hooft, ed., *The Evanston Report* (New York: Harper & Bros., 1954), p. 161.

people of God; the other is the idea of apostleship. The apostles include those who were called by Jesus, the original twelve, plus Matthias, James the brother of the Lord, and Paul—all witnesses of the resurrection. The original twelve were to be "fishers of men," who were to preach and "cast out demons" (Mark 3:14). They were promised that they would sit on thrones in the new creation, for "you are those who have continued with me in my trials" (Luke 22:28, RSV). They had witnessed the events of Jesus' life, and now they were to be his "witnesses in Jerusalem and in all Judea and Samaria and to the end of this earth" (Acts 1:8, RSV). They were warned that in their roles as teachers and leaders they faced danger, especially the danger of using the wrong kind of authority: "You know that those who are supposed to rule the heathen lord it over them, and their great men tyrannize over them; but it is not to be so among you. Whoever wants to be great among you must be your servant, and whoever wants to hold first place among you must be everybody's slave. For the Son of Man himself has not come to be waited on, but to wait on other people, and to give his life to free many others" (Mark 10:42-46, G).

Paul referred to "James the Lord's brother" as an apostle (Galatians 1:19) and claimed apostleship for himself. Paul was a wandering evangelist, who supervised the churches he had founded. He attempted to keep in touch with these churches personally, by means of emissaries, and through letters. His "care of all the churches" (II Corinthians 11:28) was one of his chief anxieties, for he had to be pastor, advisor, judge. We cannot be sure that the other apostles had the same responsibilities, but this is likely. There were some differences: the other apostles received some financial support, while Paul supported himself, and some of the others were married and brought their wives with them on their journeys.

The relation of the original apostles to the continuing ministry of the Church has been a controversial issue in all discussions of Church unity. There are those who claim that there is an unbroken succession by laying on of hands from Jesus and the apostles until now. But even Sergius Boulgakoff, an Eastern Orthodox writer, says that "we do not know in detail how hierarchy came to be established, nor can we say that it was founded upon direct 'apostolic succession' recognisable by any external signs."[4] There are others who claim that the apostolic ministry, having been based on being a witness of Jesus' resurrection, ended with the death of the apostles. They may have appointed other ministers, but not as successors.[5] Stephen Neill, himself an Anglican Bishop, rejects the view that Church and ministry depend on apostolic succession, "because we cannot recognize as Christian the doctrine of God, which seems to underlie this imposing theological edifice."[6]

MINISTRY AND HOLY SPIRIT

Davis McCaughey says that although the Holy Spirit is the spirit of order in the Church, he raised up the ministry in a way that was "extremely untidy."[7] It may prove helpful to look at some of the other ministries in the New Testament. John Knox points out that we are dealing with the functions of ministry rather than offices when we speak of prophets, teachers, workers of miracles, helpers, administrators, speakers with tongues (I Corinthians 12:38), bishops, and deacons (Philippians 1:1). These functions contributed to the ministry of God's grace and also to the running of the developing institution. The bishops and deacons, for example, were involved in administration, and possibly were identical with the administrators and helpers, or with the presidents (Romans 12:6-8). There were "no distinctions of 'inferior' or 'superior' among these workers in the churches. They were all recipients and agents of the same Spirit," and they were "equally members of the body of Christ."[8] Administration, Knox continues, was essential for planning for worship and the Lord's Supper as well as for the many incidents in the life of the community.

As the Christian community became permanent, many other functions became settled. The prophets continued to wander, but some of them settled down in one place. Teaching was

[4] In The Ministry and the Sacraments, ed. by Roderick Dunkerley and A. C. Headlam (London: Student Christian Movement Press, 1937), p. 96.

[5] See T. F. Torrance, Conflict and Agreement in the Church (London: Lutterworth Press, 1959), p. 27.

[6] Stephen Neill, ed., The Ministry of the Church (London: Canterbury Press, 1947), p. 28.

[7] Lectures at Ecumenical Institute, Céligny, near Geneva, October 1959.

[8] John Knox, in The Ministry in Historical Perspectives, ed. by H. Richard Niebuhr and Daniel Day Williams, p. 11. I am indebted to Knox's article for much of this section.

probably more prosaic than prophecy, but the prophet was often a teacher and teachers could and did prophesy. Later on, pastors and teachers were combined in one concept, as part of the local ministry, prophets belonging to a more general ministry. These were not offices but functions.

Paul did not write of elders, but they functioned after his time in churches he founded. Knox supposes that there were councils of elders governing churches by the end of the first century. In Acts we read of "James and the elders" or "apostles and elders." Elder (*presbyteros*) is the word from which we derive presbyter and priest. Sometimes elder and bishop (*episkopos*) seem to be synonymous, sometimes elders may have functioned as either bishop or deacon. The picture is "untidy."

But bishops did emerge early in the second century. Ignatius became bishop of the city of Antioch, and his letters reveal that there were bishops elsewhere but that it was not a universal practice.[9] James is sometimes said to have been the first bishop of Jerusalem, but he was the chief ruler of the council of "apostles and elders" and is to be thought of as an apostle. However, he may have been the prototype for Ignatius and others.

The New Testament does not give us a developed concept of the ministry for two reasons: first, the new community took time to become ordered and tried various ways of meeting problems; second, there was no great concern in the primitive Church for a theory of the ministry, both because the main interest was the new life in the community and because the end of the age was expected. But ministry there was! The joy of being a transformed person in the community of the Holy Spirit led to the excesses of ecstatic speaking and sometimes almost to anarchy. Order became necessary in ethical behavior, in preaching, and in worship and sacraments. Paul wrote, "All things should be done decently and in order" (I Corinthians 14:40, RSV).

A specialized ministry therefore emerged to meet the needs of the growing Church. The apostles were gone, and the leadership of the congregations fell on those of the next generation. The

---

[9] Ignatius had a high view of his office: "One must regard the bishop as the Lord himself" (Eph. 6:2). "Whoever honors the bishop, is honored of God, whoever does anything without the bishop, serves the devil" (Smyrn. 9:1). "Subject to the bishop as the grace of God, to the presbytery as the law of Jesus Christ" (Magn. 3:1). Quoted by Emil Brunner, *The Misunderstanding of the Church*, Note 2, p. 129.

end of the age did not come, and the fellowship and worship and organization needed a sound base. A separation between laity and clergy occurred as the work of the Church was regularized, for in preaching, baptism, the Lord's Supper, and administration permanent officers were necessary. This was the picture as the three-fold ministry of bishop, priest, and deacon developed in the second century.

The problem of the ministry today is bound up with the understanding of the ministry as portrayed in the New Testament and as seen throughout history. Most of the discussions of the unity of the Church founder on the crucial question of whose ministry is valid. This leads to the other problem, intercommunion, which is closely associated with views of the ministry. At the same time, there is more agreement than one might expect. The 1937 report of the Faith and Order movement reported that all Churches entrust the administration of the sacraments to their ordinary ministry. This ministry was instituted by Jesus Christ and presupposes the "royal priesthood" of all Christians. Ordination is by laying on of hands and prayer. "It is essential to the united Church that there should be a common ministry universally recognized."[10]

SACRAMENTS AND PREACHING

The point at which laity and ordained ministers are separated is in the sacraments and preaching.[11] A difference in function became a difference of order or status, and this was not a bad thing unless the Church forgot that the ministry was derived from the priesthood of all Christians and ultimately depended on Jesus Christ. Today we are agreed that the ministers are instrumental and that Jesus Christ is the chief actor and host in a sacrament, that God is not bound by his sacraments, that the Holy Spirit makes them effective, and that the minister is acting for the whole Church.[12]

These agreements have resulted from many years of ecumenical conversations. There are still varieties of opinion on each

[10] *The Ministry and the Sacraments,* p. 32.

[11] Baptism by a lay person is possible in emergency, except among Presbyterians. Lay administration of the Lord's Supper is permitted in some denominations as an act of the whole Church. Preaching by lay persons is sometimes permitted. See *The Ministry and the Sacraments,* pp. 30-31.

[12] See *The Ministry and the Sacraments,* p. 42.

point, and even in terms of vocabulary some groups prefer to speak of ordinances rather than of sacraments. Such variety is legitimate within the ecumenical fellowship, unless it leads to excommunication of one group by another.

There is no doubt that Jesus was baptized by John the Baptist, and that this baptism became the norm in the early Church. "We have all," said Paul, "been baptized in one spirit to form one body, and we have all been saturated with one Spirit" (I Corinthians 12:13, G). This was the means of becoming a member of the body, of being grafted onto the vine, of sharing Christ's death and resurrection. It was the experience of becoming a new being, a new creation, a transformed person. This was followed by the laying on of hands, which brought the gift of the Spirit.

There is no evidence that infants were baptized until sometime in the second century. Karl Barth wrote that infant baptism was a mistake and that it should be abolished, for baptism presupposes man's response as well as God's mercy.[13] Horace Bushnell, on the contrary, made out a strong case for infant baptism on the basis of his reading of the New Testament, and then proceeded to develop its theological and educational significance.[14] In either case, we can say that "the Church is the Body of which Jesus Christ is the Head, and all baptized people are the members."[15]

The Last Supper is the historic event on which the Church's sacrament of Holy Communion is based. It was called "the breaking of bread" (Acts 20:7) and "the Lord's Supper" (I Corinthians 11:20). There are many theories about its origin and its original nature. It must have been associated with a meal (whether the Passover meal or not), and it began to be separated from this love feast (agape) in Paul's time. It was sacrificial only in the sense that in the fellowship the members offered their praise and thanksgiving (hence called eucharist by Ignatius). Members of the early Church were convinced that the risen Lord was present; it was a proclamation of the new covenant; it was a foretaste of the heavenly kingdom; it was an act of fellowship;

13 See Karl Barth, The Teaching of the Church Regarding Baptism (London: SCM Press, 1948), pp. 34-54.

14 See Horace Bushnell, Christian Nurture (New Haven: Yale University Press, new ed. 1947), pp. 102-164.

15 But remember the Society of Friends; see The Ministry and the Sacraments, pp. 26, 38; see below pp. 110-114.

and it was an expression of thanksgiving. It was not mere symbolism, not simply a remembrance, not a form of magic. As a liturgical act of the congregation with its ministry, it was an experience of a personal relationship with the risen Lord, who was known in the breaking of bread and the giving of the cup through faith, that is, through the act of trust and commitment by the recipients. [16]

If we believe that Christ acts through the sacraments of Baptism and the Lord's Supper, it is equally true that he acts through the proclamation of the Word. Word and sacrament are inseparable. Preaching is one of the functions of the ordained ministry. It is primarily a proclamation of the Word, a recalling of what God has done for us in Christ, a calling of the people to serve him. In New Testament times, it was primarily an approach to the non-Christians, telling them of the "good tidings" of the love of God in Christ. When the hearers responded, teaching took place as preparation for baptism. This distinction between preaching and teaching, as developed by C. H. Dodd,[17] is helpful as a reminder of the dual responsibility of the minister, but it seems to be too sharp in terms of what we know today about communication and education. Preaching and teaching are interrelated in the modern pulpit, and both teaching and preaching are involved in the class room and in other educational activities. Where Dodd is especially helpful is in his summary of what was preached: the new age is here; this has occurred through the life, death, and resurrection of Jesus Christ; he is now the living Lord; through the Holy Spirit we know Christ in the Church; Christ will return; therefore repent and God will forgive you.[18]

The minister is ordained to officiate at the sacraments and to preach, and the Church is a congregation in which the Word of God is preached and the sacraments are properly administered. But this does not exhaust the work of the Church or of the minister. We have already seen that preaching is intimately con-

[16] See C. E. B. Cranfield, "Thank," in *A Theological Word Book of the Bible*, ed. by Alan Richardson (London: SCM Press, 1950), pp. 255-257; also see below, pp. 114-116.
[17] C. H. Dodd, *The Apostolic Preaching* (New York: Harper & Bros., 1936), pp. 3-6. See Iris V. Cully, *The Dynamics of Christian Education* (Philadelphia: Westminster Press, 1958), pp. 42-56, 114-118.
[18] *Ibid.*, pp. 38-47.

nected with teaching, that preaching is missionary in its original outlook, and that ministry involves service in the Church and in the world. These activities can take place effectively only when there is creative administration, and from the beginning this was part of the work of ministry, shared perhaps by laity and ordained ministers. This points to the significance of the minister as a leader, endowed with authority, and when we look back on Paul's ministry especially as revealed in his letters, we find that he was a man with authority over the congregations he had founded and that he sent forth his helpers to assist in spotting and overcoming difficulties. Against this background, we can agree with H. Richard Niebuhr in his concept of the minister as a "pastoral director" or "leader of leaders."[19]

When the difference between lay person and minister was one of function, the sharing of a common ministry was more or less obvious. But now that it has become one of status or order as well, it is difficult to establish the proper relationship. I have heard clergy discuss the ways they can *"use"* their lay people, forgetting that the people *are* the Church, and that the Church expresses itself in the world through the laity. Furthermore, when the laity become concerned about the Church, they are likely to burden themselves with "church work" instead of "the work of the church," being exhausted by activities within the congregation instead of being witnesses as Christians in their daily work.

There needs to be a balance between the laity and the clergy in carrying on the work of the congregation, and there also needs to be a balance between the lay person's obedience to Christ within the congregation and in his daily life. If the minister is to be a "pastoral director," he must not rob the laity of their "royal priesthood" at either point. Too often, the clergy are exhausted by doing work in the Church which should be done by lay people; and just as often the demands of the local congregation make it impossible for the lay people to take positions of significance in terms of Christian leadership in their daily lives.

Further confusion is seen when the Church seeks to act or speak in secular affairs. J. H. Oldham's warning is important here: "Action by the Church may in practice mean several en-

[19] H. Richard Niebuhr, *The Purpose of the Church and Its Ministry* (New York: Harper & Bros., 1956), pp. 79-94.

tirely distinct things. It may mean action imposed or recommended by the authorities of the Church. It may, on the other hand, be intended to refer primarily to action by the clergy. In this case, a further distinction has to be made, i.e. whether what they do is done in their capacity as office-bearers of the Church or whether they are acting as individuals or private citizens. Or again, the action intended may mean action by the Christian laity, either in faithful discharge as Christians of the duties of their vocation, or as associating themselves for the achievement of particular social and political ends, the pursuit of which they believe to be demanded by loyalty to the Christian profession. When the laity so act, they act, or ought to act, as members of the Church, though not as its official representatives. All these forms of action are quite different from one another, and failure to distinguish between them and the unreflective use of the general term 'church,' to cover wholly distinct forms of action, has perhaps been one of the principle hindrances in the way of a true and fruitful understanding of the functions of the Church in the social and political spheres."[20] Against this background, we can speak of the teaching ministry of the Church.

THE CHURCH'S EDUCATIONAL MINISTRY

Before looking at the teaching ministry of the laity, we need to be reminded of one other group. Hendrik Kraemer refers to the "clericalized laity," who exist in "the secluded world of the Church." They are protected from the pressures of the secular world and yet they are in a congregation which is to a great extent secularized. They are in a position, says Kraemer, to protect the Church from secularization and to open the Church to the world. They are not a third order but are laity, and therefore they, like the rest, must stay in dialogue with the world. There are educators, musicians, secretaries, maintenance men, and others on the staffs of our congregations who fit into this special category of "clericalized laity" and who therefore have a special responsibility to help the Church in its proper relation to the world.[21]

In many ways the ministry of the lay person is being expressed. The Reformation as such did not help very much, but

---

[20] Quoted by Ph. Kohnstamm in *Church, Community, and State in Relation to Education* (London: George Allen & Unwin Ltd., 1938), p. 164.

[21] See Hendrik Kraemer, *A Theology of the Laity*, pp. 165-166.

among Congregationalists, the Friends, and the Methodists, for example, lay people have had opportunities both within and outside the Church to serve more fully. In all Churches, there has been an increasing emphasis on lay participation in Church government. As far back as 1780, the Sunday school movement began among lay people and in many congregations today it is still a lay movement, although sometimes in the bad sense of being separated from the Church. A lay thrust into the ecumenical movement came from the Student Christian Movement. Women's groups, from the local to the national level, are almost entirely lay led. The World Council of Churches has become concerned about this issue. The issue of laymen's work was brought into sharp focus when Madeleine Barot, who had done Christian work through the French underground during World War II, was asked to head a division of women's work. She saw clearly that this was not one of the essential categories of the Church's work, and as a result of many discussions the World Council established a department of the laity which she heads.[22]

In Evanston in 1954, the report of the World Council of Churches said that "it is through its lay membership that the Church enters into real and daily contact with the workaday world and shares it problems and aspirations. It is in the life and work of the lay membership that the Church must manifest in the world its regenerative and redemptive power. One of the greatest tasks of the Church today is to grasp clearly the significance of the lay ministry *in* the world."[23]

The Christian's vocation is to witness to his faith in Jesus Christ. He does this through his worship and his activities in support of the Church, but his effective evangelism is in the world. The living room, the train, the snack bar, or wherever conversations take place, often provide opportunities for discussion.

Chiefly this witness is through what men *are* rather than what they do or say. But one's true being is supported by his acts and his words, or else he is a hypocrite. We are the recipients of a new being which makes possible what we do and say. Because

22 See Howard Grimes, *The Church Redemptive* (Nashville: Abingdon Press, 1958), pp. 42-45; Gabriel Hebert, *God's Kingdom and Ours* (London: SCM Press, 1959), pp. 150-151.

23 *The Christian Hope and the Task of the Church* (New York: Harper & Bros., 1954), "The Laity—The Christian in His Vocation," p. 1. Quoted by Grimes, *op. cit.,* p. 45.

of what Christ has done for us, *now* are we sons of God, and so we act in the world. Only we do not do this consistently, and we need to turn to the Lord in penitence and for the renewal of our strength.

The lay person's ministry shows itself in service. In spite of the deprecation of the "do-gooder," the Christian lives in terms of the story of the Good Samaritan. Many lay people find their vocation in social service, in medicine, in counseling, in teaching, in police work. But often they feel that they are alone in an area of work which has been secularized, and the Church as an institution does not provide them with the opportunity for fellowship along vocational lines. When lay people are professionals in such fields, the pastor may call upon them for the use of skills he does not have. There are many others without special skills who fulfill their ministry in their day-to-day work simply by having an attitude toward others which communicates something of the love of God. The opportunity offered by the Roman Church through the Lay Apostolate in its ministry to the poor is an example.[24]

Sometimes a lay person has an opportunity to act in a prophetic way. Joseph Fletcher recounts the story of Edward Stettinius, Sr., who was president of the Diamond Match Company at a time when most kitchen matches were poisonous. If the poisonous matches were outlawed, it would give the Diamond Match Company a monopoly because of its exclusive control of a nonpoisonous match. The dilemma was solved when the Diamond people released their patents for general use.[25] William James used to talk about the "nitro-glycerin" of the Gospel, which could blow up the ways of the irreligious.

The ministry of the laity finds its great opportunity in teaching. The Christian parent is involved in this task simply by being a parent. The parent brings or does not bring the child to baptism or dedication. During the early years of childhood, the parent is in complete control. The education that occurs is mostly in the unconscious, but it is crucial for the child's future. Faith, expressed in attitudes and atmosphere, is contagious, just as anxiety and dread are contagious. The training of parents for

[24] See "Launching a Lay Apostolate," by Catherine deHueck Doherty, *Religious Education* (Nov.-Dec. 1959), LIV, 502-504.

[25] "The Ministry of the Laity," published by Episcopal Theological School, 1945, p. 15; *The New Yorker*, January 27, 1945.

this task is of paramount importance to the Church as well as to its children. Here is a problem of Church policy which must be worked out by clergy and laity working together. The parent maintains some control of his child's schooling, sometimes including the choice of a state or private or church-related school. He has much to say also about the continuation of that schooling and the direction it will take.

In the schools, the Christian teacher has the opportunity to witness to his faith, although there are degrees to which this may be prohibited on the verbal side. The professional teacher who is a Christian, as he teaches in any school or college, is faced with opportunities of tremendous importance. The sense of community within the school is essential for the nurture of the pupil, and this is just as significant as the technical knowledge he acquires. It is not something which is taught in courses on moral and spiritual values or religious instruction, but it is an atmosphere of concern for the spiritual welfare of persons which permeates the life of the school in its total curriculum: the whole of the experience for which the school has responsibility.[26]

There are other forms of teaching not always considered as such. The large body of youth workers, playground directors, parole officers, and others who have opportunities to work with young people in their out-of-school time are influencing these people. This is education, often of a more indelible nature than what happens in school. The basic assumptions about morality and the significance of other persons often develop under the tutelage of such people. When they are Christians, the opportunities for witnessing to their faith are frequent.

Within the Church as an institution, we find those who are charged with the responsibility to educate their pupils to be the Church. The kind of community life offered by the Church when it is true to its heritage is of paramount importance. Lay people, whose work is in the world, are able to help those who are immature to know what it is to live as Christians in the world. Here is where the Biblical faith can overtly be brought to bear on the problems of daily life as the pupils see those problems. Here is where the lore of the Church's tradition comes alive as their own history, where they see that, as God has been at work in history, so he is still Lord of history. There must be

[26] See W. R. Niblett, *Christian Education in a Secular Society* (New York: Oxford University Press, 1960), pp. 22-32.

a genuine dialogue between the learner and the teacher if any significant learning is to take place, and this dialogue must be based on a relationship of mutual trust. It is possible to achieve this relationship only when the Church is a community of the Holy Spirit in which God's grace is channeled through its members. Such a community is never completely achieved.

The teacher can do something about this. Reuel Howe suggests that there are five essential characteristics of the Christian teacher. First, he seeks to incarnate the Holy Spirit rather than teach certain subject matter; he is sensitive to the meanings which the pupil brings and to the relationship between himself and the pupil. Second, he seeks to recognize the freedom of the learner to be himself and to stand beside him in his search for the realities of Christian faith. Third, he is willing to wait and to trust the Holy Spirit as the pupil works at his own speed, with only occasional attention along the way. Fourth, he is not anxious about the methods he will use; he has many methods at his command and he adapts them as the situation develops. Fifth, he believes that as revelation is always personal, so also there is a person-to-person (I-thou) relationship in which communication can take place and revelation can occur.[27]

Wesner Fallaw has come to the conclusion that we cannot expect lay people to achieve proficiency in teaching religion. This task, he believes, should be restricted to the ministers and a few highly trained lay people. Such a program, if the additional people could be recruited and trained, would provide excellent weekday training in religious knowledge, similar, perhaps, to what is achieved in the schools of England, Sweden, and West Germany. But I believe that it reduces the ministry of the laity at a point where it should be expanded. The genuine nurture which leads to Christian commitment and continuing growth in grace occurs within the congregation of believers, and through the relationships of Christian life we come to new insights into the relevance of the Gospel for daily living. In this area, the teaching ministry of the laity is essential.[28]

So far, we have been speaking of the ministry of the laity in

[27] Reuel L. Howe, "A Theology for Education," *Religious Education* (Nov.-Dec. 1959), LIV, 494-495; see below pp. 76-80, 189.

[28] See Wesner Fallaw, *Church Education for Tomorrow* (Philadelphia: Westminster Press, 1960), pp. 13-23. See also James D. Smart, *The Rebirth of Ministry* (Philadelphia: Westminster Press, 1959), pp. 84-104. For a complete reassessment of the clergy-laity relationship, see Arnold B. Come, *Agents of Reconciliation* (Philadelphia: Westminster Press, 1960), pp. 98-124.

education. But in the development of the ministry in the New Testament, we saw that the relation of preaching and teaching was such that neither one could exist independently. The great commission is that we should "teach all nations." The minister is "to teach, and to premonish, to feed and provide for the Lord's family." He is to "instruct the people." The minister is to be a teacher in the same way as the laity. At this point, they share the same ministry. But the clergyman has another responsibility, which is to be the trainer of teachers. Here he shares a responsibility with the whole Church, for we do not yet have a sound educational theory of what it means to educate people to be the Church. But the minister cannot wait for this to happen, important as it is. He needs to develop his own skills and theory in terms of the immediate need. He needs to give priority to his educational ministry, so that the Church's lay people can turn their devotion into effective teaching.

We have seen that the Church is the people of God. In the community of the Holy Spirit, the first ministers were the apostles, and other ministers were distinguished by differences of functions and not status. As the Church developed, the ministry changed from untidiness to tidiness, and by the beginning of the second century there was a ministry of bishops, priests, and deacons. In this ordering of the life of the Church, however, the priesthood of believers constituted the body of Christ, and the works of preaching and sacraments and administration remained the special function of the ordained ministry, although the clergy had other significant responsibilities as well.

Our concern, against this background of the Church's ministry, has been the specific teaching ministry of the Church, a responsibility shared by the ministry of both laity and clergy. When we know what the Church is, we can see the goal of what we intend when we educate people to be the Church, but we still need to discover the educational resources within the life of the Church as a community. The faith of the Church turns on factual knowledge of historical events and their interpretation, as well as on the significance of the life of the Church as it is lived in community. To these problems we now turn.

CHAPTER III

The Church's Teaching

WE HAVE seen that the Church is primarily a community of the Holy Spirit. It is the people of God, and all of the people share in the Church's ministry. Yet in the total life of the Church there are functions which are reserved for the ordained ministry. Held in common as a duty of both the laity and the clergy is the teaching ministry, especially in terms of education to be the Church. Education takes place in community, and the sharing of faith is also the communication of belief. The Church's teaching involves factual knowledge, interpretation, and incorporation of attitudes into the lives of the learners.

We cannot think seriously about Christian education without becoming involved in theology, which might be defined as *the truth-about-God-in-relation-to-man*. But our task is not simply to teach theology; it is to use theological insights in such a way that the learner comes into a vital relationship with God within the community of the Holy Spirit. So we can say that the slogan of Christian education is: *Theology in the background: grace and faith in the foreground.*[1] Theology guides the process, but is not identical with the process. The education which occurs is due to the dynamic factors of interpersonal relationships within the community, through which the Holy Spirit is active as the love of God at work. Within such a relationship, the living Christ is known as redeemer and savior, the human personality

[1] In *The Clue to Christian Education* (New York: Charles Scribner's Sons, 1950), p. 7, I wrote *"Theology in the background: faith and grace in the foreground."* The change in word order is significant; it places the priority of God's grace in relation to man's faith in the proper position. See also my *Education for Christian Living* (Englewood Cliffs: Prentice-Hall, Inc., 1956), pp. 60-71; Daniel Day Williams, "Current Theological Developments and Religious Education," in *Religious Education,* ed. by Marvin J. Taylor (Nashville: Abingdon Press, 1960), pp. 44-53.

grows toward wholeness and becomes more and more integrated in relationship to the living reality of God in human experience. The new creation, which is a gift of God, is not only formed but is nourished and nurtured by life in the community, and thereby gains strength to live in the world. But dynamic functions must have guide-lines, growth must have goals, insight must have expression, and the revelation of God must be translated into verbal symbols and be systematized for intellectual purposes. If God in Christ is the focal point of Christian education, we must know who God is and who Jesus Christ is. We need theology in the background.

From theology we derive in turn the truths which need to be imparted, the direction which growth in grace should take, and the methods and goals of Christian education. When theology is relevant to life, it is capable of providing what is needed for a sound Christian education. It provides certain essential beliefs about the nature of God's creation, about the nature of history, about the nature of man, about the destiny of man, about God's kingdom.

REVELATION

This theology is something we have inherited, and yet it is the development of our own minds. It is based on revelation, primarily as this revelation is recorded in the Bible and centrally in Jesus Christ. Revelation is something which God does to make himself known to man. An event takes place, and a man sees the meaning of that event. God does something, and a man is led to see God in what has happened. A centurion watched as Jesus died, and saw the truth: "Truly this man was a son of God!" (Mark 15:39, RSV). The disciples looked back on all the occurrences which they had witnessed: Jesus' life, teachings, death, and resurrection; and they began to see what this meant. "This Jesus," preached Peter, "God raised up, and of that we are witnesses. Being therefore exalted at the right hand of God, and having received from the Father the promise of the Holy Spirit, he has poured out this which you see and hear. . . . Let all the house of Israel therefore know assuredly that God has made him both Lord and Christ, this Jesus whom you crucified." (Acts 2:32-33, 36, RSV). Here is a summary of the manner in which Jesus was revealed as Lord to the apostles. The Gospel was proclaimed by Peter, and to the hearers also it became a revelation, for they were "cut to the heart" and they repented and were baptized.

The view which one holds of revelation affects his view of Christian education. If I believe that what is revealed is God's own words, given verbally in the Scriptures, then my interpretation of Christian education would be to learn as many of these propositions as possible, preferably in God's own words (or even own tongue). This view easily leads to the teaching of doctrines as ends in themselves, although this frustrates the main idea, for even if revelation occurs in propositions it is conceived as "saving" truth rather than intellectual belief.

If revelation is the breaking through of God into history at a moment in time, and if theology is the interpretation of this moment, Christian education may be discarded as something unimportant. For if the only hope of man is that God may speak to him at another moment, education may become a form of blasphemy, for it is seeking God where he cannot be found. Proclamation is the only hope, and the proper purpose of education is to inform those who are already converted.

If revelation is something which goes on all the time, as God acts through the events of history and daily life, and if God's supreme revelation of himself is what he did in and through Jesus Christ, then Christian education has a dual purpose: we need to know the facts about the events as well as their interpretation for the illumination of the meaning of God in our lives today. Here we recognize the priority of God's grace, but the response of faith within the dynamic community of the Holy Spirit is part of the total picture. Through life in the community we are enabled to remember the event which is at the center of God's revelation, and it becomes a continuing reality in our experience. Thus history and tradition become essential to the educational process. But what we are working for is decision and not intellectual assent. The act of faith or trust in God is something that cannot be controlled by the educational process, but the conditions can be set up.

THE FOCAL POINT

For the Christian, Jesus Christ stands at the center of history as well as at the focal point of his faith. These two factors are intertwined, for Jesus came in "the fulness of time" to be the means whereby God reconciled the world to himself.[2] It is hard to be sure what Jesus himself thought of his ministry and purpose. It is likely that he did not use or accept many of the titles subsequently applied to him, but that he saw his task as a unique calling to be a prophet and to declare the meaning of the coming kingdom to his people. The important point, however, is that thinking about him developed in such a way that the full value of his life and death and resurrection became evident to the apostles and to the early Christian community.[3]

Just as the Church is described by many titles, so Jesus was known by many names. In his lifetime, the most common were prophet, teacher, master, rabbi. He may have referred to himself as Son of Man, with a unique meaning, and he may have used the term, bride-groom, in a messianic sense. But most of the terms of theological significance were applied after the resurrection, the most important being Lord. The term, Christ, which means Messiah, soon lost its significance and became a name for purposes of identification, with or without Jesus as part of it.[4]

Not only Lord but many other terms seemed appropriate to the New Testament community: Son of David, the King, the Judge, the Shepherd, the Savior, the Mediator, the High Priest, the Lamb, the Image of God, the Light of the World, the Way, the Truth and the Life, and the Word.[5] These names referred to a man whom the community remembered as a human being and whom they knew as living Lord.

Their memory of him as the man of Nazareth was significant in their interpretation. We can never get far from the historical Jesus portrayed in the Gospels as we think about our Lord and Master.[6] He came preaching repentance and the coming of the kingdom of God. The kingdom would come quickly, and the

[2] See my interpretations in *The Clue to Christian Education,* pp. 18-36; *Biblical Theology and Christian Education* (New York: Charles Scribner's Sons, 1956), pp. 83-111.

[3] See John Knox, *The Death of Christ* (Nashville: Abingdon Press, 1958), pp. 33-123.

[4] See Vincent Taylor, *The Names of Jesus* (London: Macmillan & Co., 1953), pp. 5-71; see also, Ian T. Ramsey, *Religious Language* (London: SCM Press, 1957), pp. 137-144, for "Son of Man."

[5] See Vincent Taylor, *ibid.,* for 42 such names.

[6] I have tried to picture Jesus through the eyes of a boy in *I Remember Jesus* (Greenwich: Seabury Press, 1958). See also John Knox, *The Man Christ Jesus* (New York: Harper & Bros., 1941) and *Christ the Lord* (New York: Harper & Bros., 1945).

kingdoms of this world would be replaced by the direct rule of God. There was an urgency about his preaching and this led to a sense of watchfulness. But in another sense the kingdom was already here, for there were those who were already under God's rule; furthermore, his healings were a sign of the presence of the kingdom. He was acting as the central figure in the announcement of the kingdom, for God had sent him to fulfill this role. But the kingdom did not come, and opposition to his ministry led to his death. Left behind was a ministry in which he was the perfect example of that which he taught, a rich legacy of ethical and religious teachings, and a band of distraught followers.

The early Church remembered what Jesus had done, but they also knew him as living in the present. Their only approach to the meaning of Jesus was through the resurrection and the gift of the Spirit. In Jesus as Lord they saw the fulfillment of the Old Testament expectation of the coming of the Messiah and the end of the age. This was not the consummation (for Jesus would come again), but in principle it had been established through the formation of the Church by the activity of the Holy Spirit. Jesus was known as Lord by the community, based on the memory of the event and the experience of the Holy Spirit.

Norman Pittenger makes a suggestion which shows the importance of the community. "Let us suppose," he writes, "that in the days after the Resurrection, perhaps at the time of the Fall of Jerusalem, the entire Christian fellowship had been wiped out by Romans or by Jews. Let us suppose that the documents which had been written about Christ during the intervening half-century had been hidden in some secret place—like the Dead Sea Scrolls, perhaps, in a cave where they would be safe from marauders. Christianity would not have existed after the destruction of the community and the hiding of its documents. Then in our own time, let us suppose, archaeologists discover the documents. They translate them, make them available to the general public, and thus bring before the eyes of the modern reader the figure of Jesus—both as Man of Nazareth and as the One believed to have risen from the dead, and known as such in the literature which reflects the first days of the now non-existent fellowship."[7] There would be no Church, and Jesus would have

[7] W. Norman Pittenger, *The Word Incarnate* (New York: Harper & Bros., 1959), pp. 57-58.

about the same reality as the "teacher of righteousness" in the Dead Sea Scrolls. Such a discovery would not create the Christian community in the twentieth century.

This points to the significance of the Church as the carrier of the Gospel and as part of the Gospel. The Church is always visible and can be seen in its members. It is both the local congregation and the visible unity of congregations, so that the local congregation is representative of the universal Church and the universal Church is found in the local congregation. The Church is the temple of the Lord. "So then you are no longer strangers and sojourners, but you are fellow citizens with the saints and members of the household of God, built upon the foundation of the apostles and prophets, Christ Jesus himself being the chief cornerstone, in whom the whole structure is joined together and grows into a holy temple of the Lord; in whom you also are built into it for a dwelling place of God in the Spirit" (Ephesians 2:19-22, RSV).

The Church is part of our faith in Jesus Christ. This is an inescapable fact of history. If we say that we can know Christ through the Bible, this is true only because the Bible is the Church's book, its history, its memory. If the Bible were like the Dead Sea Scrolls, it would not convince anyone unless it were supported by the believing community.

THE BIBLICAL FAITH

The Bible is the Church's book, and the Church is utterly dependent on the Bible for the record and memory of its faith. The Bible contains all that is necessary for salvation, and the Church is not to teach anything contrary to scripture. The Bible carries authority not because of its legal power or its expert knowledge; the source of all authority is God, but the seat of authority is peculiarly in the Bible. The Bible is interpreted by men, and even John Calvin distinguished between what was absurd and what was valid.

The Bible's authority is not external to the Church. It is not a series of propositions, and we need to remember that revelation is a coincidence of a particularly revealing event and a mind illuminated by grace to see the meaning of the event.[8] The Bible is the record or the story of God's creative, redemp-

[8] See William Temple, *Nature, Man and God* (London: Macmillan & Co., 1934), pp. 315, 499, 500.

tive, and sustaining activity in history, reaching its climax with the coming of Jesus Christ, and continuing in the life of the Church; this story is found in the Bible and *nowhere else*.

This does not mean that the Bible is infallible or inerrant. The discoveries of recent years have enhanced the authority of the Bible by establishing its uniqueness, and this was made possible by overcoming the old claim that it had legal, expert, or infallible authority. Because we are freed from literal accept- ance of immoral acts as part of God's will and of the apocalyptic imagery as a literal interpretation of the age to come, we are enabled to see more clearly the total impact of the record of the mighty acts of God.

Certain statements about these developments are helpful. "First, the authority ascribed to the Bible must not be inter- preted as prejudging the conclusions of historical, critical, and scientific investigation in any field, not excluding that of the Biblical documents themselves." Second, "Christian thinkers are not necessarily bound to the thought-forms employed by the Biblical writers." Third, "the Biblical writings display a wide variety of literary type. In using the Biblical books as a standard of authoritative teaching, these facts must be taken into ac- count. The supreme spiritual value of some parts of the Bible is not shared by all." Fourth, "in estimating the relative spiritual value of different portions of the Bible, the standard is the Mind of Christ as unfolded in the experience of the Church and ap- propriated by the individual Christian through His Spirit. That is to say, the stages of the Biblical revelation are to be judged in relation to its historical climax."[9]

We begin our interpretation where we stand, which is within the Biblical story as members of the Church. We keep our attention on the center of the story, Jesus Christ, who is "the pioneer and perfecter of our faith" (Hebrews 12:2, RSV), "our leader and example in faith" (G). In our understanding of Jesus Christ, we are enabled to see the unity of the Old and New Testaments. But we know Jesus Christ as the living Lord within the Church, and therefore we see the Bible from within the liturgical and doctrinal positions of the congregation and denomination wherein we stand. There is room for such dif- ferences within the body of Christ, provided we begin with

[9] William Temple, ed., *Doctrine in the Church of England* (New York: Macmillan & Co., 1938), p. 32.

loyalty to Christ as our chief allegiance. This is what we find today in the World Council of Churches, which is not a super-church but a means whereby the divisions of Christ's body can be brought into relationship.[10]

The compelling power of the Biblical faith can be seen when we understand it as an unfolding drama of redemption.[11] It may be true that we should call the incarnation the "crowning of creation" and that it would have occurred even if there had been no sin, as Norman Pittenger suggests,[12] but the fact remains that man did and does sin and did and does stand in need of being restored to the right relationship with God and his fellow creatures. Every man has been created, has come under the covenant of law, has failed to hold to his side of the agreement and therefore has stood in need of reconciliation as this is promised in Christ, has needed community in order to become a person and can find it in the Church, and faces the consummation at death. This is the story of every man, and it is also in barest outline the story the Bible tells about man and God.

The Bible unfolds the story of God's creation. Man's response is ambiguous and usually negative, beginning with the story of Adam and Eve. But God does not give up, although we can see his doubts about man in the story of Noah, and the broken communications in the story of the tower of Babel indicate that the community of man is in a perilous state. These primitive stories are revealing because even in prehistory we can see the struggle between man and God. Man's freedom is unquestioned, but he does not use his freedom to obey God.

The drama moves on to the story of the covenant. It begins with Abraham, and again as we read of events in the dark past we discover God's willingness to forgive and his desire to establish Abraham as the father of Israel. This is not due to Abraham's righteousness but to God's mercy. The same story continues in the time of Moses, with the covenant now expressed in terms of the Law. This Law becomes the major element in the lives of the Hebrews, but the prophets point out that God's

[10] See my treatment of authority in *The Clue to Christian Education*, pp. 170-183; *Biblical Theology and Christian Education*, pp. 191-209; "Authority, Scripture, and Tradition," *Religion in Life*, Autumn 1952, pp. 551-562.

[11] See Bernhard W. Anderson, *The Unfolding Drama of the Bible* (New York: Association Press, 1952).

[12] W. Norman Pittenger, *The Word Incarnate*, p. 252.

righteousness is offended by Israel's unfaithfulness. Hosea makes it clear, however, that even when Israel plays the harlot, God will forgive her unfaithfulness. Against the background of the glories of the kingdoms of David and Solomon, of the miseries of exile and being a subject people, faith in Yahweh is maintained, but it takes the insights of the Second Isaiah to see the meaning of God in the sufferings of the people. Many other themes work themselves into the covenant story, but God's agreement with his chosen people remains dominant. There is the promise of the coming of the Messiah and of the offering of a new covenant.

The next stage is the coming of Christ and the making of the new covenant. He comes both as the crowning of creation and as the turning point in history. "God proves his love for us by the fact that Christ died for us when we were still sinners" (Romans 5:8, G). Here is the revelation of God's love at work in sacrifice, and through this act of God in Christ a new relationship is established. In *Dr. Zhivago,* Yura writes of his half-brother: "For the second time he has burst into my life as my good genius, my rescuer, resolving all my difficulties. Perhaps in every life there has to be, in addition to other protagonists, a secret, unknown force, an almost symbolic figure who comes unsummoned to the rescue, and perhaps in mine, Evgraf, my brother, plays the part of this hidden benefactor?"[13] Christianity is the story of a rescuer. The hidden benefactor may seem to be my brother or my friend or someone unknown to me, but behind every human benefactor lies the saving love of God in Christ.

It is this Christ who continues to be at the center of the stage in the next act, the coming and continuance of the Church, which is the body of Christ and the community of the Holy Spirit. In this community are those who have made a decision for Christ and who now become hidden benefactors of those in need. Here is the point at which we enter the Gospel story, we become members of the body of which Christ is the head, and we appropriate to ourselves the story of redemption. Through the worship of the Church, through its preaching, prayers, and the Lord's Supper, we keep in communion with the Head and have the power to live as his disciples in the world. In this sense only we can call the Church a redemptive

[13] Boris Pasternak, *Dr. Zhivago* (New York: Pantheon Books, 1958), p. 287.

and redeeming community, because God is the one who acts for our redemption and who maintains our communion with him.

There is a final stage to the story the Bible tells. It does not stop with the Church, for the kingdom of God promised in Scripture has not yet come to pass. In part it has been realized in Christ himself and in the coming of the Holy Spirit, but there is always the promise of the end, in terms either of the second coming of Christ or of the final coming of God's kingdom. This view needs to be separated from its first century imagery if we are to find that it has value for us today, and already there is a hint of a new direction of thought in the Fourth Gospel with its theme of "eternal life." Paul put it this way: "It is plain to anyone with eyes to see that at the present time all created life groans in a sort of universal travail. And it is plain, too, that we who have a foretaste of the Spirit are in a state of painful tension, while we wait for that redemption of our bodies which will mean at last we have realized our full sonship with him. We are saved by this hope, but in our moments of impatience let us remember that hope always means waiting for something we haven't yet got. But if we hope for something we cannot see, then we must settle down to wait for it in patience" (Romans 8: 22-25, P). Here is the source of our hope in the face of death and judgment, in the face of the expectation that in God's own time he will bring in his kingdom, and in the anticipation that all things come to an end. Because Christ is Lord, we are freed from anxiety. As Luther translated John 16:33, "In the world you have anxiety. But be confident, I have overcome the world."[14]

The Biblical story faces man with the necessity for a decision. It is a story which comes alive in the life of the Church and is reflected in many aspects of the Church's liturgy, its Church year, and its structuring of the life of its members. "The Bible," writes Paul Tournier, "is the book of choice. From end to end it sets man face to face with the supreme choice which determines all the other choices of his life; from the law of Moses: 'I have set before you life and death . . . therefore choose life,' to the words of Christ: 'No man can serve two masters.' In each of the personal dialogues of which the Bible is full, the Word of God

[14] See my *Biblical Theology and Christian Education* for a full development of this interpretation of the Bible and the way it can be applied to the teaching of various age-groups.

speaks to man, making him a person, a responsible being who must answer. The Bible stresses the inexorable and radical nature of that choice: from the Old Testament, where the prophet Elijah cries: 'How long halt ye between two opinions?' to the Revelation: 'Thou are neither cold nor hot: I would thou wert cold or hot.' "[15]

SOME GOALS OF CHRISTIAN EDUCATION

Lewis J. Sherrill, in one of the most significant books on Christian education, *The Gift of Power,* dealt with the problem of the nature and goals of Christian education in a way consistent with the theme of this book. He wrote that "Christian education is the attempt, ordinarily by members of the Christian community, to participate in and guide the changes which take place in persons in their relationships with God, with the church, with other persons, with the physical world, and with oneself."[16] It is concerned with the total person and takes place within a Christian community where one may normally expect some confrontation with God to occur. It is the kind of education which bears witness to revelation and leads to some response from the learner.[17]

Our educational processes are the *means* to the ends, and Sherrill was careful to keep this distinction clear. We can control these means to some extent. We can make sure that there is the opportunity for one to gain factual information about the Bible and Church history and the doctrines of the Church, to be included within the community as a recognized member, to hear that a personal response to revelation is needed, to receive counsel when it is asked for, and to be invited to make one's own decision. These are areas in which we can act effectively, provided the atmosphere is such that the pupil's motivation to learn is stimulated. But a great deal of Christian education stops at exactly this point. We are often satisfied with the impartation of religious knowledge, and expect that people will be changed by what they know. If we are not satisfied with this approach, we then seek to encourage them to make a decision, and this is often a form of

---

[15] Paul Tournier, *The Meaning of Persons* (New York: Harper & Bros., 1955), p. 210.

[16] Lewis J. Sherrill, *The Gift of Power* (New York: Macmillan Co., 1955), p. 82.

[17] See *ibid.,* pp. 89-90.

manipulation, whereby the youngsters of a certain age are confirmed or make a profession of faith or join the Church. If these things happen, we may conclude that perhaps this congregation is not the *koinonia* described in the New Testament.

Sherrill suggested the following ends or goals: "that persons might be drawn into the kingdom of God; that they might attain to increasing self-understanding and an increasing realization of their own potentialities; and that they might sustain the relationships and responsibilities of life as children of God."[18] These goals are in terms of our understanding of the nature of the Church as the *koinonia*. The important thing is membership in the community of the Holy Spirit, where one can recognize the claim of God on his life in relationship to other persons. This membership is a gift through baptism and yet in time it requires a commitment which must be freely made to be valid. One is enabled to make a decision only as he understands his maturing self and discerns the source of his increasing integration or unification. In the light of such a decision or series of commitments, growth in grace becomes a possibility; one takes his place in the Christian community and in the world as a witness to the love of God as revealed in Jesus Christ, with all the difficulties and joys which this vocation promises.

This whole process turns on one's awareness of the heritage of the Christian community and one's knowledge about and of Jesus Christ. In nothing that we have said is there any discrediting of factual knowledge and its interpretation. Theology always stands behind the grace-faith relationship, guiding the process, subjecting it to criticism, and pointing afresh to the goals. The problem is to provide factual information and its interpretation so that it is psychologically and spiritually valid for the learner. It is hard, sometimes, to realize that the way in which factual knowledge becomes meaningful in one's life is not in terms of systematic and logical presentations, not in abstract formulae, not even in attractive stories. Factual knowledge must always be relevant or within reasonable probability of becoming relevant for it to be meaningful.

Have you ever been asked to look at a picture of a group of children you do not know? Curiosity may make you take a cursory glance. If you know they are the children of a distant rela-

[18] *Ibid.*, p. 83.

tive, you may look more closely to see if they resemble anyone in your family. If they are the children of a family who moved away just last year from your immediate neighborhood, you will enjoy the picture to the degree that you knew the children. But if they are your own children, you will cherish the picture and look at it many times. The significance of the same factual presentation in the picture depends on our relationship to what it represents.

Too often the pictures of Bible characters are like the unknown children in the photograph. Most of us today can see more significance in the Queen of England than in the Queen of Sheba. It is hard to get excited about ancient kings when we elect presidents. Until one gets inside the Bible story and can identify himself with the persons portrayed, the factual information is not going to have any religious value.

We are forced back to the significance of the community. The quality of life of the congregation provides the framework for appreciating the facts upon which the Church is based. When I am able to apprehend that this history is the history of *my* people, that *I* am a participant in the continuing history of God's people, I can begin to see the significance of some of the facts, and I can begin to distinguish between the two tribes of Israel about whom it is worth while to know something and the other ten tribes who drop out of sight. I begin to understand that some kings and queens and prophets are relevant to the way of living experienced in the congregation, and these may stand out while the others I may forget. But all of this I see within the overall framework of a drama of God's mighty acts in history, including my history.

In such a way factual information may be taught. In children's earlier years, this means that facts which are inherently interesting to children must be selected for that reason, but that they must also be seen to have relevance in terms of our knowledge of their religious needs. Because we can understand their situation, we seek for those parts of our story which will illuminate and make meaningful their own daily experiences. They need to hear of God in terms that will enrich their relationships with God and other people, so that they will participate within the limitations of their immaturity as fully accepted children of God within the community.

It is our hope that those who are educated to be the Church

will come to a point of decision. They will ratify and confirm their baptismal vows, or they will believe and be baptized, and they will be accepted as full members at the Lord's Table. Here again we must be careful about manipulation, which is subtly present simply because we have a confirmation or members' class at a certain age. On the other hand, we must be sure that they hear the invitation, and this can be missed if they have already dropped out of the community.

Often confirmation or any other adolescent act of decision becomes a form of "graduation." It is a release from the Church school program, or from the classes in religious instruction. Into this vacuum the young confirmand is thrown, and so he quits. Many churches have a place for him in a "youth group," and he never finds his way there. He has often decided for confirmation or its equivalent because this will take the pressure off and he can do as he pleases; and this does not include going to Church.

Some think the answer to this is through changing the age of confirmation. Because early adolescence is a period of instability, let us have him confirmed at ten, so that the gifts of grace coming from the sacrament will help him through this difficult period. Let us postpone it until fourteen, so that he will have some information as a background for understanding his decision. Let us do away with confirmation and have a profession of faith made after he is eighteen, with at least two years' instruction. Let us postpone confirmation until eighteen, in spite of all the pressures from parents and all the social customs surrounding it, say some West German Christians. Let us admit them to Holy Communion at twelve, with proper preparation, and then have confirmation after eighteen on the basis of adequate instruction, is another suggestion.

It is not my intention to investigate the merits of these suggestions, for it seems to me that they all fall short of the mark. In so far as the Church is the *koinonia,* the children know themselves members of a community of the Holy Spirit, and in this community they know that they are accepted as they are, that the rules of the community apply to them with equal fairness, that the others are interested in them personally and give them every opportunity to grow at their own speed, and that within the community they sense, however vaguely, something of the holiness of the almighty God who dwells in the hearts of his people. If this were achieved sufficiently so that children could sense it, we could confirm infants with the Orthodox or not at all with the Friends.

But decision there must be. Horace Bushnell wrote of "little conversion-like crises" which go on all the time. "The Spirit of God is never so dove-like as he is in his gentle visitations and hoverings of mercy over little children." We do not need a "spiritual tornado" but we do need decisions to trust in God so that we may grow in the spirit.[19] We know that these decisions are going on all the time, and that as growing children face the anxieties of life they need the guiding hand of someone who loves them and whom they can trust. In such a manner God's love is mediated to them and they come more and more to trust the God of Jesus Christ as they find him in the family and in the Church.

But the task of Christian education is broader than the Church or the family. Christians live in the world as disciples of Jesus Christ, and this is infinitely harder than expressing that discipleship in the Church. We come back to the dual theme of the laity in the Church and in the world. The Church exists in the world and must always remain in some kind of dialogue and relationship with the world. To this problem we now turn.

[19] Horace Bushnell, *Christian Nurture* (New Haven: Yale University Press, new ed., 1947), pp. 329, 330.

CHAPTER IV

Church and World

THE Church exists in the world. Because it is centered in the God of Jesus Christ, it is also centered on the God of Abraham, Isaac and Jacob. God is the creator and is the Lord of this world. We are not in the Church in order to escape from the world, but because we believe that as we worship God we should serve him in this world. It was said of the early Christians that "they remain on earth, but they are citizens of heaven."[1] This dual citizenship makes one a more responsible creature within God's creation, a better neighbor, a more loyal citizen, and a more effective workman. But the situation is broader than the activities of individual Christians. We are told that the Church is to have power to overcome wickedness among the principalities and powers. The life of the Church is to have an influence on society in general, including its economic, social, and political functions. It is concerned with family life, educational standards, working conditions, and international relations.

The Old Testament is built around the idea of covenant, and this means that God acts in history and that man stands under obligation to fulfill his part of the agreement. The Biblical view of revelation is clear in its portrayal of God as one who makes himself known by his action in history. He may be displeased with Israel's response, but "be assured then, that it is not because of your goodness that the LORD your God is giving you this fine land to occupy; for you are a stiff-necked people" (Deuteronomy 9:6, G). The point is that God is concerned with the people, the nation, and, as the view is expanded, with all mankind. When Amos starts listing the sins of the nations, he goes

---

[1] "Address to Diognetus," 5:9, *The Apostolic Fathers*, translated by Edgar J. Goodspeed (New York: Harper & Bros., 1950), p. 278.

right down the line: Damascus, Gaza, Tyre, Edom, the Ammonites, Moab, Judah, and Israel.

> "Because they have sold the innocent for silver,
> And the needy in exchange for a pair of sandals;
> They who trample upon the heads of the poor,
> And thrust aside the humble from the way" (Amos 2:6-7, G),

God holds a plumb-line in the midst of his people, for what he desires is that justice may roll down as waters and righteousness as a perennial stream (Amos 5:24). Even after the exile, Israel maintains its faith, for it sees that the exile is the result of its misdeeds. The nation expresses its corporate penitence, going back in its history to Egypt, where they disobeyed, to the Red Sea, where they rebelled, to the camp of Moses, where they were envious, to the worship of the molten image, to their refusal to believe Yahweh's promise of a pleasant land, to their sacrifices of sons and daughters to the idols of Canaan, and to the destruction of the kingdom. In each case, God had forgiven them, and now they pray,

> "Deliver us, o LORD, our God,
> And gather us from among the nations,
> That we may give thanks to thy holy name,
> That we may glory in thy praise" (Psalm 106:47,G).

The New Testament never loses its continuity with prophetic religion. Just as the prophets know God must act, so the New Testament faith is based on God's action in bringing his kingdom into being. This kingdom will overcome all the distinctions, evils and suffering of this world, for it will be ruled by love. We are not told how this kingdom will come or what its structure will be. We do not know the time of its coming, but the expectation is that it will be soon. Here is no radical plan for social reform, but a simple commandment to love, because God first loved us. When this requirement of love is applied to the community, it becomes a radical principle (not a plan) of reconciliation and mutual concern, as expressed in the first century experiment in communal holding of the treasury. Here, then, is the germ of a social gospel, and it means that we must put first things first in this world. Here the prophetic teaching of the Old Testament is transformed by a deeper personal element.[2]

The other factor in the concept of the kingdom of God is that it is to some extent realized here and now. But the realization is not something that happened in Palestine and then stopped. It is a recognition that God is at work in this world now, bringing his purposes into reality through the work of men. This is God's action in history, and the Church as the fellowship of the Spirit accepts responsibility for its part in the process. P. T. Forsyth put it this way: "Our Lord did not come to save souls, or to gather devout groups, or even to found churches, but so to save souls and found churches as to make Christian nations and thus change society to the Kingdom of God."[3]

The world is God's creation, as is the Church. There is nothing about the world *as such* that opposes it to the Church, but within the world there is that which can be called anti-Church, or anti-Christ, or the kingdom of evil. In the sense that Christ came to redeem the world, the Church is concerned for the redemption of that in the world which is opposed to the purposes of God. The Church has no absolute rules for approaching the problems posed by the world. It has to work from the implications of the Gospel, and these may vary with the situation. "It is precisely from the historical perspective given in the Old and in the New Testament (Romans 9-11) that the Christian knows that God's command sounds different to different men at different times," wrote Martin Dibelius. "The nature of the Christian life is based on *faith, love, and hope*. This means that it consists in radical obedience, superhuman love, and treating everything that exists as relative and provisional."[4] From this perspective we can speak of the sins of society and the sins of the Church with the corresponding need of corporate penitence. Both Church and world stand under judgment, but the Church under God has a responsibility to the world.

[2] See Ernst Troeltsch, *The Social Teachings of the Christian Churches* (London: George Allen & Unwin Ltd., 1931), I, 51-64.

[3] "A Holy Church the Moral Guide of Society," *The Examiner*, May 11, 1905; quoted by E. R. Wickham, *Church and People in an Industrial City* (London: Lutterworth Press, 1957), p. 201.

[4] Martin Dibelius, "The Message of the New Testament and the Orders of Human Society," in *Christian Faith and the Common Life* (London: George Allen & Unwin Ltd., 1938), pp. 39, 33.

RAPID SOCIAL CHANGE

There is much talk today about the challenge to the Church of the process of rapid social change. The Church is pretty much still oriented to a pre-industrial or even a feudal society. In some countries it has come to terms with democratic processes and has even adopted them in its own polity. But it has never really captured the imagination or loyalty of those who have been most affected by changes in society. It has been maintained by a comfortable majority of the population who have provided nominal support, or by the fiction that the nation as a whole is the Church's membership, or by a militant minority who have positions of leadership and can be heard in the formation of national policy.

Whether it has reached the masses of the people, at least since the industrial revolution, is doubtful. In England, as early as the sixteenth century, there was the practice of "pewing-up" of parish churches; pews were either owned outright (and sold from time to time to the highest bidder, or included as part of the property when a house was sold) or rented. With very few free seats available, the poorer people would not take part. Already the process whereby the unskilled laborers lost interest in the church had begun! But even where most pews were free, they were not occupied.[5]

What was worse, the bishops were on the side of the propertied and the conservatives, and there was great bitterness against them, especially in the manufacturing districts. Chiefly, asked Thomas Arnold, "is it not because in our large manufacturing towns the church has allowed thousands and tens of thousands of its members to grow up in misery and in ignorance; and that a step-mother's neglect is naturally requited by something of a step-mother's popularity . . . ?"[6] It was a period of fatalism and resentment, and it is estimated that in the city of Sheffield, England, two-thirds of the adult working class were estranged from the churches by 1840. Only about one-third of the children had any schooling; most of them worked and had no time for school or Sunday school. Life was hard and short, with the mortality of

[5] See E. R. Wickham, *Church and People in an Industrial City*, pp. 41-46.
[6] Quoted by E. R. Wickham, *op. cit.*, pp. 86-87.

children especially high, but it was much easier for the upper classes.[7]

Bishop E. R. Wickham, in his book on *Church and People in an Industrial City,* has much more to say on the alienation of the working classes in Sheffield, England, but the point is that the rapid social change brought in by the industrial revolution was accompanied by the failure of the Church to meet the needs of the people. A hundred years later the change had accelerated, but perhaps nothing was as catastrophic as the beginnings which we can observe at least in one industrial center in the eighteenth and nineteenth centuries.

When we turn to the twentieth century, in the industrial field, we see many more changes, especially with the coming of great factories and automation. This leads to a greater depersonalization on the job, but often there are more opportunities for personal relations and development in home and community. For many, however, there is a degree of marginal living which is almost as miserable as that described in eighteenth-century Sheffield. Urban living provides many conveniences but intensifies many difficulties in personal relationships. People live longer, and this opens up a whole new area of problems concerning the "population explosion."

The churches have not been able to cope with these changes, and this has led to a continual dropping off of Church membership in proportion to population in many countries. Industrialization has come to be understood as the general technological development which has occurred in practically every field of labor, including agriculture, transportation, mining, and other endeavors. From the Christian perspective, it is seen as a gift of God to be used for his purposes. Therefore, Christians need to

[7] This can be illustrated by the average death rate in Sheffield in the years 1839, 1840, 1841:

	years
Gentry, professional persons and their families	47.21
Tradesmen and their families	27.18
Artisans, laborers, and their families	
a. Trade and handicraft	21.57
b. Manufacture	19.34
Paupers in the workhouse	25.51
Farmers and their families	37.64
Agricultural laborers and their families	30.89

Quoted from *The Claims of Labour,* Sir Arthur Helps, by E. R. Wickham, *ibid.,* p. 92 n.

understand the economic, sociological and technical factors, and to seek those forms of social and political action which will deepen the life of the community, nation, and world. This kind of thinking requires the skills and resources of members of all churches, such as has been going on in the World Council of Churches since its formation and in the ecumenical conferences on social problems which began in 1925 in Stockholm.

There are many other problems posed by social forces and movements not related to industrialization. Problems of land reform, of the peasants and tenant farming, of the rise of large cooperative farms (under both capitalism and communism), and the breakdown of rural society are concerns of the churches. The collapse of colonialism, so closely connected with missions, and the rise of nationalism, often both anti-Western and anti-Christian (the two are identified in the minds of the nationalists), offer a threat and a challenge to the Church. The rise of anti-Christian states, especially communism as it spreads from Russia to other countries, threatens religious freedom and makes it almost impossible for the Church to have any influence in the social field except as a kind of rear-guard action.

As individual Christians face these facts of social life, the response is likely to be one of bewilderment. Only as all the resources of the Churches are brought together can there be developed a sense of direction and action. We are convinced that "God calls us to act in society, making use of economic and political structures and movements which are available instead of waiting until there is an ideal situation. The certainty of His victory frees us from illusions and false hopes, and at the same time guarantees that in whatever circumstances we find ourselves our efforts will have significance in God's ongoing purposes for society. . . . Questions of the 'spirit' cannot be separated from questions of the 'body'. . . . Questions of individual ethics, of family, of the goals of economic life, of human rights, and of international cooperation can never be answered in isolation from each other."[8]

[8] *The Common Christian Responsibility Toward Areas of Rapid Social Change* (Geneva: The Department on Church and Society, Division of Studies, World Council of Churches, 1956), pp. 5, 39; see also, *Statements of the World Council of Churches on Social Questions* (Geneva: The Department on Church and Society, Division of Studies, World Council of Churches, 1956).

THE RACE PROBLEM

Many volumes could be written on the relation of Church and world. It is our purpose here only to sketch the picture by way of illustrations. The race issue has become sharper as a result of the rising nationalism of many areas, of the policy of *apartheid* in South Africa, and of the 1954 Supreme Court decision in the United States. Although it is true that in Christ there is neither East nor West and that all races are one in Jesus Christ, the question is complicated by historical, social, and political factors. The judgment of God on racial discrimination is quite clear from the Biblical record and the prophetic note needs to be sounded not only from the pulpit but in any discussion of Christian ethics.

The chief source for the condemnation of current customs is within the Church. It is here that the sin of discrimination can be recognized for what it is. The community of the Holy Spirit is open to all mankind, and in so far as the local congregation seeks truly to be the Church there can be no question of exclusion on racial or any other grounds.

But members of churches, clergy and laity alike, tend to approach racial problems in terms of customs or policies based on secular and political assumptions, without regard to the demands of the Christian faith. This makes it almost impossible for leaders in the Church, whether clergy or lay, to face the problem on their own terms, even if they see the problem as an internal one.

In this situation, education is a starting point. It can be the means of seeing the claim of God on the members of the Church, even though it runs the risk of offending others within the body of Christ. This has been the position taken in most of the resolutions at denominational meetings, but only rarely have these resolutions been implemented at the local level. The World Council of Churches has used the same approach with the Church in South Africa. Within the Christian brotherhood, such discussions should be possible without endangering the relationships of the members.

But the situation is not this simple. In one situation, the ministers had spoken against segregation prior to the Supreme Court decision of 1954, but the action of the Court gave them an opportunity to express their approval of the action. The state schools were closed to prevent integration and immediately pressures were brought to open the church buildings as private segregated schools. Most of the lay people were afraid to vote against this policy, and permission was given to use the churches. But there were some laity who at serious risk to their businesses and social standing refused to be silenced, including the editor of a local weekly paper, a clerk in a store who was threatened with the loss of her job, owners of businesses who would not discharge Negro employees, and teachers who believed in the public schools even at the cost of some degree of integration.[9] In this situation, the clergy assisted by a minority of their lay people made their witness. So far events have gone against them, but the end of the story has not been written.

This was both an internal and an external problem. There were strong influences both within and outside the churches to accept the segregation pattern throughout the community. The churches had not solved the problem within their congregations, and could not be expected to withstand the political and social and economic pressures from the outside.

The Negro churches are not seeking integration within their congregations, but they are capable of facing the outside world with a demand for integration. The witness of Martin Luther King, backed by many Negroes and some whites, is an example of a Christian approach to the race problem from the side of those seeking justice for themselves. In this case, the discipline of non-violence is combined with courage and forthright action. Such an approach has won the admiration of all but the most extreme segregationists.

Until the churches put their own houses in order, they are not going to make a strong impression on secular customs. The evidence of genuine multi-racial congregations is extremely meagre, so that even the fact that a congregation advertises itself as "interracial" is considered news. The Church has failed to mix the races as much as it has failed to mix the classes of society. This is not to say that congregations should not contain like-minded people, which is a natural grouping and often to be desired, but the claim of the Church is that it excludes no one on the basis of race, class, or caste. The crucial test of a congregation is whether it can operate across the lines set up by society.

[9] See "Background Information for Church and Society" (Geneva: Department of Church and Society, Division of Studies, World Council of Churches), December 1958, pp. 1-7, mimeographed.

Only then can it make its witness felt in the realm of race relations. But even from the weakness of its present state, it must make as effective a witness as possible.

POLITICAL ISSUES

When one crosses the border from the west to the east sector of Berlin, he immediately becomes aware of a difference in the social climate. Although conditions in East Germany have improved economically and socially and the political regime is more securely established, one still senses the grimness of the faces and the colorlessness of its life. Citizens have become resigned in the face of what seems to be a permanent partition of their country, and the steady stream of refugees to the West continues, especially among the intellectuals.

East Germany is almost completely Protestant, and it is now under a Communist regime. Should Christians accept involvement in the regime or should they keep their distance? Should a Christian farmer cooperate in a communal farm, and what attitude should he take if he does? Should the Church fight all the restrictions or not? What should students do about the oath which involves accepting the basis of dialectical materialism?

One way out is to analyze what one means by loyalty, as Karl Barth has done in his letter, *To a Pastor in the German Democratic Republic.* It is not blind loyalty, he says, and a person may have "certain unvoiced reservations," including the right of "freedom of thought over against the ideology, and the right of opposition, even to resistance to particular implications and applications of the given system. There is such a thing as loyal opposition. He is 'loyal' to a given form of government who recognizes its validity and authority for himself and is resolved to accept it within the limits of what is inwardly and outwardly possible to him. I would not see any difficulty, were I in your shoes, offering this loyalty to the East German Republic, and thus in truthfully pledging the oath that is required from you."[10] Barth believes that this oath is different from the one required by Hitler, and yet even voting in an election may involve approval and not just assent.

[10] Karl Barth, Johannes Hamel and Robert McAfee Brown, *How to Serve God in a Marxist Land* (New York: Association Press, 1960), p. 68. See also "Background Information for Church and Society," March 1959, pp. 13-14 (World Council of Churches, Geneva).

The central issue turns on the Communist youth dedication (*Jugendweihe*). The softer approach became more severe in 1959: "If you have not taken part in the *Jugendweihe,* then you can't be a part of our state, there is no place for you in an academic secondary school, and it is even doubtful whether you will get any chance at a trade or other vocation." This automatically applies to the children of pastors. It is the alternative of confirmation and comes at the same time: fourteen years of age. The Church so far has held fast to the incompatibility of confirmation and *Jugendweihe,* so only a small number are now being confirmed. It can only hope that the previous instruction in religion, now held in free time outside of school but still attended by a majority of the children, will have some value in the future.

It is felt by many responsible Church leaders that such a decision is too much to demand of a fourteen-year-old. One group within the Church now suggests the abolition of confirmation, along with the recognition that baptism is what makes one a member of the body of Christ and therefore eligible to receive Holy Communion. Confirmation, they say, is not based on the Bible, and furthermore it has not been effective in holding the young people. Here is an example of a re-thinking of both theology and of the ways of the Church as a means for finding a way to live in a society opposed to Christianity. The solution adopted in 1960 is the reduction of the age of confirmation to twelve years, so that confirmation will precede the problem of youth dedication.

In such a situation, the Church has to improvise. It becomes difficult to train ministers. The *Haus der Kirche* in the east sector of Berlin is able to train young girls for Christian vocations, under the watchful eye of the state, but it cannot provide any secular knowledge and therefore must restrict its teaching to the Bible, theology, church history, and music. Even the religious instruction given in free time comes under the supervision of a state inspector who can examine the pastor or catechist to determine if he is fit to teach the youngsters, but in 1960 this right was not being used, although the inspector did grant the license.

Another group of East German Christians realizes that the Church is always facing hazards and temptations. Ideological conflict, they claim, is not as important as conflict over facts, and even then the Church must allow freedom for personal decision on the part of its members. The problem is to discover where to say, "no," and then to do so whatever the cost may be.[11]

The East German situation is relevant because the Church there is now working out a means of living with a totalitarian state and is still vocal. The lines are drawn, but they have not become crystallized. The Church and the state can still converse, and as a result changes in policy do occur. This is partly because the Church speaks from strength, including the resources of the Church in the West.

For the Christian, the communist state is part of God's world. On the other hand, a government where the head of state is head of Church is a secular state. We do not have a "Christian" state, but only a state in which a certain number of people are incorporated in the body which is the Church. The major motives of every government have a secular basis. It has always been calamitous when a churchman has had supreme political power, and it is not the job of the Church to tell the state how to run its business. But the Church can enter into conversation with the state, and it can, for example, show why it is opposed to the *Jugendweihe.* Or state and Church may cooperate on an issue and together may try to convince the people that segregation is wrong. Or the Church may confess its own sins in the matter of its failure to work with the people or the state in facing the problems raised by the industrial revolution. Or the Church may seek to analyze the conditions which are leading to rapid social change and to map out plans for alleviating the evils and appropriating the goods for the people as new nationalisms emerge. In such cases, the Church must seek for its own unity in the Gospel and then in the expression of this unity point in the direction it believes the will of God requires, remembering always the freedom of the Christian conscience for its members and the relative nature of all ethical decisions. God still speaks to different men and nations in different ways, for he is primarily a God of grace rather than of law.

EDUCATION AND THE WORLD

We come now to the implications for Christian education of what we have said about the Church and the world. In this time of rapid social change, we cannot rely on the power of tradition

---

[11] See "Background Information, etc.", *op. cit.*, pp. 11-17.

or of the moral values inherent in our society. There are corro-
sive forces at work, accelerated by two world wars, and there are
mighty constructive forces hidden in the scientific advances of
our age which we do not yet understand. Many attitudes in our
society are based on certain natural virtues, such as honesty and
justice and wisdom, which are inherited from the Greeks rather
than from the Jewish-Christian tradition. They existed in the
Stoic philosophy and they are found in the secular traditions of
the enlightenment. But these virtues, too, have been shaken by
these wars. In Germany during Hitler's time an enlightened
liberalism could not withstand the onslaughts of a totalitarian
state while a confessing Christianity could do so.

The starting point of all Christian education might be described in terms of a formula:

— from the world — to the Church — to the world

The pupil comes from the world, with whatever natural virtues
and other insights into values he may have; he brings with him
himself, with his anxieties and problems and searchings; he
comes out of an environment which has to a great extent formed
him: home, school, work, recreation. He is all of the things he
has done, and much more inside himself that is hidden from
himself and from others, except God. He comes from the working
classes, from a racially outcast group, from a totalitarian state,
from an anti-Christian school, from work in which he finds little
meaning. He may have roots deep in a set of secular values; he
may have roots in a rich family history; he may have no roots at
all. He also comes as a unique individual, different in some way
from everyone else in the congregation or in the class. And yet
he is a person, a creature of God for whom Christ died, one who
has unique value in the sight of God. But this last point he has
not learned; he may have heard it said, but he has not experienced the reality of it.

So he comes from the world to the Church. Here he finds a
community of the Holy Spirit, a fellowship of Jesus Christ, a
people of God. At least, this is what the local congregation hopes
to be in so far as it has heard the Word of God. Here he can
bring the myriad of his experiences which have made him what
he is, and in this fellowship he is enabled to search for the meaning of his existence. Here he gains a perspective by which he may

evaluate his experiences. Here he gains a framework for making value judgments on his activities and thoughts. Here he finds out what it means to be a member of the working class, as far as God's purposes are concerned; here he finds out what it means to live as a Christian and yet be cast out of segregated schools. Here he learns what it means to live according to the secular values around him and he becomes able to distinguish those values which are consistent with the insights of Christian faith. Here he discovers that his roots are deeper than family or nation, and that his own history is involved in the history of God's people. So he comes into personal fellowship with other persons within the community and is enabled to take upon himself the gift of the new relationship offered by the redemptive love of God in Christ. At this point, however, he is faced by a decision: the gift of the new being comes from his faith in Jesus Christ. This decision becomes unavoidable, and it affects his total person and all his past, present, and future relationships.

The heart of the matter lies in this question of decision, and this does not rest primarily on information. There is no examination of factual knowledge which determines whether a person is ready to be a "deciding" Christian. It is not that knowledge is unimportant, for we know that it is of tremendous importance, but it is not the crucial question. The crucial point is this matter of loyalty, of a loyalty to Christ that gives one a perspective on whatever knowledge he may have. A moron can be a Christian, provided he has that minimum of wit necessary for responsible decision; and it is my guess that by God's grace all are accepted by him who in their frailty are incapable of making any decision at all (for else what would we say of a loving God when infants die and when Mongolian idiots have a life with a minimum of self-consciousness?).

Decision rests more on meaning than on accumulation of facts. Whatever we have in our experience which we bring with us from the world into the community of the Holy Spirit is grist for the mill of Christian education, for our task is to see these experiences in terms of the will of God for us in our lives. Nothing is meaningless, although many things may seem so when they are contrary to what we believe to be God's will. The Gospel illuminates this life as well as transforms it.

Decision rests on discernment, and again discernment is not so much knowledge as it is light breaking through. As we bring our experiences and those of our fellows to the presence of God in worship and discussion, the light dawns and we discern God's will in the midst of all the relativities of life. When we have discerned God's claim on us, we are enabled freely to make a commitment, if we will.

There is "one Lord, one faith, one baptism, . . . but grace was given to each of us according to the measure of Christ's gift" (Ephesians 4:5,7, RSV). Some are called to one task and some to another, but all are equally members of Christ's body. It is in this sense that information is essential. There is no excuse for ignorance of the teachings of the Bible and the Church; there is no excuse for ignorance concerning the meaning of vocation, or of the facts behind the crucial decisions of our society. Knowledge is a qualification for action as a Christian, rather than for the decision to be one; and this knowledge depends on one's capacities and calling. The crime of the Church is that it does not have or does not provide the kind of knowledge its members can use in order to be intelligent citizens in this complex world of rapid social change. The Church does not make use of its tremendous resources to discover why it lost so many of the working class, or why it was unable to stop the corroding action of moral relativism, or why it was unable to find a satisfactory alternative to communism among certain peoples. The Church has not provided the information we need to be intelligent about atomic energy and its ethical consequences, about the international tensions of the cold war, or about the rising nationalisms of subject peoples. The Church did not provide for itself sufficient information about its foreign missionary program to anticipate the radical changes forced upon it in the middle of the twentieth century. Frequently the Gospel seems to be a light submerged in a muddy stream of ignorance rather than a beacon light directing the transportation on a mighty river.

We have said that the learner comes from the world to the Church, and there he is exposed to the redemptive love of God within the community of the Holy Spirit. Within this fellowship, he is given what knowledge he can absorb, although his commitment is based on discernment and not on information. But in order to use this act of faith in the service of God he needs the intelligence service of the Church. This includes not only that knowledge which will make him at home with the heritage of the community but also that knowledge about the changing world which will enable him to act as a Christian citizen. Because he has found the meaning of his life within the educational procedures of the Church, he knows that as a member of the Church he must carry his insights back to the world.

This, ideally, is what should happen to every child and adult. As he learns to discern the hand of God beneath the surface of events, he is able to interpret his world from a different perspective. How he acts will be determined by the conditions, and these conditions can be very complex, involving not only his livelihood but also the security of his family. He may find that some kind of compromise is necessary in order to survive at all, or at least to survive in a way that will provide meaning for his work or his family life. It may cause him to be cautious in a situation of racial tension, or to move slowly in the face of the demands of a totalitarian state. But it does not provide an excuse for cowardice or for denying his faith in Christ in terms of some other loyalty. He has not only the conviction that God is an ever present help in trouble (Psalm 46:1), but ideally that the Church is supporting him in his loyalty and will understand him in his failure.

A child comes to the Church with his problems. He may be having trouble in school, or some playmates may have teased him on the way to church. These are important experiences deserving the attention of the teacher and the meaning which can be derived from the Biblical faith. In this way, we can understand something of the frustration which a child experiences and the need for living with it if it cannot be overcome, or the sinfulness of one's self and his playmates which stand in need of forgiveness from God and man. Here within the fellowship there is direction and strengthening which the child can take with him as a light into the world where such experiences will be repeated.

Boys and girls often need courage to stand up for their loyalty. A story is told by Sir George MacLeod of the tiny roofed chapels in Winchester Cathedral. "Only one retains its original completion of gilded boss and carved foliage: that of William of Wykeham. All the rest were more or less despoiled by the riots of Cromwell's day. The story goes that a mob had brought to confusion every praying place and chantry and were gathered to despoil this last, only to discover one of their own officers guarding, with drawn sword, William's shrine. The man was a Wykehamist, apprehended in the main of Cromwell's cause yet equally convinced that ancient things had power. 'Strangled by his old school tie'—or its Cromwellian equivalent—may well have been the comment of many in the mob: but the majority must have understood. The place was saved."[12] The Christian is like that man, ready to work with new and even radical ideas, and yet to retain the basic faith as an element in the future.

As youngsters grow up, they are searching for the meanings of their experiences: boy-girl relationships, sex, marriage, work, education. The Church has light to throw on these things. As the youngsters bring their perplexities to the light of the knowledge provided by the Gospel, they are enabled to see new meanings and to use them as they return to their everyday life.

But young people not only bring the problems of their own lives, they begin to see also the perplexities of the world itself. They begin to ask the question, "Why doesn't the Church do something about it?" About the problems of juvenile delinquency, about unmarried mothers, about the race problem, about the atom bomb, about the communists, about political morality? Whatever has caught their attention in the newspapers or in discussions with friends or at home is relevant. They need the social gospel in the same way as their elders do. They need access to the sources of responsible information, guidance in how to interpret it, and help in utilizing it as Christians in the world. It takes courage for a young person to speak out against what seems to be a majority opinion, especially when the issue involves emotions and traditions. Young people do not court unpopularity. Yet there are young people in East Germany who choose confirmation in preference to the youth dedication of the communists, and take the consequences in terms of no further education and poor jobs and sometimes even loss of promotion for the fathers. The race issue brought out similar courage among the teenagers in Little Rock, Arkansas.

The job of the teacher is not to provide "Christian" answers to such questions. We have said that God speaks in different ways to different people at different times. But the opportunity must be provided through adequate information for them to "hear" what God says to them. Dr. Kohnstamm reminds us that "Christian education is the action of one who is aware that he can never become the ultimate source of authority for another,

[12] *The Christian News-Letter.* No. 99, September 17, 1941.

but that he *can* make him feel that both of them alike stand before the only real authority, that is, the authority of God."[13]

Christian education is something that continues all the time. It is a matter of learning more, of enriching one's life, of deepening one's loyalty, and of acting more intelligently and courageously in terms of the understanding of God's will in this time and place. We come from the world to the Church and then return to the world.

[13] Ph. Kohnstamm, "Christian Education in the World of the Present Day: Its Nature and Its Mission," in *Church, Community, and State in Relation to Education* (London: George Allen & Unwin Ltd., 1938), p. 139.

CHAPTER V

The Church and the Congregation

"I BELIEVE in the holy Catholic Church, and regret that it does not exist," said an eminent churchman. To which the reply was made that the holy Catholic Church had been seen in action at Edinburgh, Oxford, Madras, Amsterdam, and Evanston, where Christians of all communions came together because they accepted Jesus Christ as God and Savior. There is a sense in which the visible catholicism of Christianity is found in the ecumenical movement.

"I believe in the holy Catholic Church, and regret that it does not exist," but it can be replied that the holy Catholic Church can be found in this place, in this congregation, here and now, because the parish seeks truly to be the community of the Holy Spirit, to be in communion with all disciples of the Lord, and to be universal in its outreach to the world. "I believe in the holy Catholic Church *in this place*," can be said by clergy and laity alike when they see what the nature of the Church is in the local congregation. To achieve this goal requires re-examination, self-criticism, and a re-thinking of the New Testament picture of the Church in terms of the twentieth Century.

THE SITUATION TODAY

In 1953, John Heuss preached a sermon on "The True Function of a Parish." In it he commented on the programs in the average American congregation, deeply involved with maintaining a well-housed organization. "What most parishes are habitually doing is so prosaic and so little related to anything except their own hand-to-mouth existence that the public cannot imagine in what way they can possibly influence the great affairs of the world." In these congregations the people work hard, but what has come out of it is a new doctrine of the Church, which he characterizes as follows: "To many people the Church is a pleasant community activity where one's children attend Sunday School, where adults go occasionally, and where one goes during the week to meet other nice people and raise some money so that the Church can stay open. On Sundays the parish is a religious institution. During the week it is a series of promotional, organizational and semi-commercial activities. The Gospel proclaimed on Sunday finds no translation into the relationships of the weekday."[1]

When we look at the local congregation, what do we see? Here is the *Church of the Elder Son,* made up of respectable people who keep the law; they put more emphasis on clean clothes and proper mannerisms than on the care of the poor; they emphasize the importance of good works, but realize that things must be kept in balance. It almost becomes "the country club on its knees."

Closely related is the *Church of Immaculate Perception,* in which the impeccable building is used by people who are sure of their doctrines; the worship is often like a drill-team in action; there are no surprises but there is strict discipline; there are class rooms for the children, with chairs and tables the proper size and books with beautiful bindings which may be handled with care.

Even more familiar is the *Church of St. Simon the Magician.* It takes its name from the story in Acts, in which Simon asks Peter for the secret of his healing power and offers to pay him for it. Peter's answer is unforgettable: "To hell with you and your money! How dare you think you could buy the gift of God?" (Acts 8:20, P). But this congregation has not heard Peter's answer; it believes that one can buy himself into the kingdom of God. It is proud of the number of men in the congregation who are in the upper salary brackets. It has a large and well-trained staff, and there can be no doubt that the library has the best books that money can buy. To the preacher, they say,

> "Speak to us smooth things,
>   prophesy illusions" (Isaiah 30:10, RSV).

There is also the *Church of Apostolic Succession.* It believes that there is no other Church. It has the only true doctrine going back to the apostles, or the only true form of the Church, or the only valid ministry. The scandal of Christendom is not that there are so many churches, but that every church is not like

[1] John Heuss, *Our Christian Vocation* (Greenwich: Seabury Press, 1955), pp. 5-6, 7.

it. This congregation has not heard the letter of James: "You believe that God is one; you do well. Even the demons believe —and shudder" (2:19, RSV).

There are many other churches, but one more must be mentioned. This is *St. Millstone-by-the-Pond.* This is the place where the people do not like children. Children are treated as second-class citizens; they are not allowed in the main worship, for they might disturb someone and possibly tear a hymnal page. "After, all, there isn't five dollars in all of them!" Jesus said, "Whoever causes one of these little ones who believe in me to sin [or stumble], it would be better for him if a great millstone were hung round his neck and he were thrown into the sea" (Mark 9:42, RSV).[2]

TRUE FUNCTION

The only place where one can find the church pictured in the New Testament is within the local congregation. The word *ekklesia* was applied with equal validity to the Church as a whole and to the local congregation. John Heuss has described a local congregation in New Testament times. It had, he wrote, five distinguishing marks:

First, there was a vivid sense of the soul-shaking experience of knowing Christ. The apostles had known Jesus in the flesh, and after the resurrection they knew him as their living Lord. Within this community, they had been transformed, and as new creatures they sought to witness to their faith.

Second, their fellowship was distinguished by the genuineness of their trust in God through Christ. In the light of the promised coming of the kingdom of God, they did not worry about their own preservation but only about achieving God's will for them. Fear and anxiety were banished and replaced by the experience of God's grace.

Third, they knew their fellowship to be a Spirit-filled community. Pentecost was a dramatic portrayal of the power of the Holy Spirit. "The early church was like a beehive in reverse. There was much coming in and going out; but the coming in was to get renewed strength from fellowship, prayer and the Breaking of Bread in order to take the precious Word of salvation out to the uttermost parts of the earth."[3]

[2] See "The Church's Nature and Christian Education," in *The Christian Educator,* January-March, 1959, pp. 7-10.
[3] John Heuss, *op. cit.,* pp. 10-11.

Fourth, they were aware of having had their sins forgiven. Freedom to act was a real possibility because they were no longer shackled by the sense of anxiety, dread, and guilt. Because they were no longer separated from God, they were free to serve him.

Fifth, they valued organization only to the degree that it helped them in the achieving of their goals. Organization was necessary for worship and teaching and taking care of the needy. One did not become a member by joining a committee but through the experience of a changed relationship with God and one's fellows.

On each of these five marks, Heuss comments that in the modern congregation we see something less than what was normal in the early Church. These five basic qualities, he says, "have largely disappeared from our parishes."[4]

There is one other difficulty which might be called "the monster parish." It exists in Germany in terms of geographical boundaries, where as many as 25,000 will be considered members of the parish. The same may be true in England. In America we read of the "successful" parish with its 8000 members. In 1861, a clergyman named Samuel Earnshaw claimed that smaller church buildings and parishes of under 400 homes would be helpful. "People cannot now be converted on a monster scale. . . . As long as we have only monster parishes there will be apathy and standing aloof of the people. They will not be visited by their parochial minister, because he cannot personally visit so many; they may be absent from Church too, but he does not know who is absent because his church is a monster church; and they may in their hearts desire to receive counsel and comfort from him, but he cannot know the state of their minds, neither if he did, could he comply with their wishes, because his parish is a monster parish."[5]

RENEWAL OF CONGREGATIONAL LIFE

One starting point of any kind of renewal is the selection from within the membership of some people with genuine insight who will meet together and ask certain basic questions. These are

---

[4] John Heuss, *ibid.*, p. 12.
[5] *The Church and The Artizan:* Sermon at the parish church of Sheffield, England, Feb. 10, 1861, by Rev. Samuel Earnshaw; quoted by E. R. Wickham, *Church and People in an Industrial City*, p. 152.

questions which will help the laity to understand their ministry. Heuss suggests three questions:

"What is the true religious job of this parish?" Here is the opportunity to turn to the nature of the Church as we find it in the New Testament, and to see how it functioned and what its goals were. The group begins to evaluate their own congregation in the light of these functions and goals. What happens is that they see where they have been missing the mark in what they were trying to do, because they were placing their effort behind the wrong kind of endeavor.

"How can all that is done in this whole parish set that true religious task forward?" This second question can only be asked meaningfully against the background of the first one, although sometimes the questions can start with: "What does this parish do?" and then "Is what this parish is doing contributing to the purposes of the Gospel?" In either case, the group comes to the point where it needs to define "the Church in this place" in terms of their understanding of the New Testament. They can begin to see, from this perspective, the place of the Church in the world and of their parish in their neighborhood. They can grasp something of the ecumenical nature of Christianity and struggle with the relevance of the ecumenical movement to their own lives. They may decide that many of their activities in the parish have nothing to do with the kingdom of God; they may conclude that they have introduced secular values into parish life rather than let parish life permeate the values of the secular community.

"To what extent is everything which we are doing changing the lives of the people involved?" Perhaps this question can be answered personally by the members of the group. They need, however, to evaluate the parish activities as such, asking what proportion of the members respond to an activity, why they claim to participate, what happens to them when they become seriously involved, and what impact this activity ultimately has on the secular community.[6]

The group that takes part in this kind of congregational self-examination will be likely to provide lay leadership of a new kind. The new insights will be accompanied by greater loyalty and more intelligent action. But they must be ready to have these

[6] See Charles D. Kean, *The Christian Gospel and the Parish Church* (Greenwich: Seabury Press, 1953), pp. 57-69.

insights rejected by members of the congregation who have not been through the process, and sometimes by the pastor. In some cases they will discover that their offer of leadership is not desired. This is a natural reaction by those who are both comfortable and insecure in their religious life. However, the group can become the leaven in the lump.

Out of this group may emerge a select few. They may become what John Heuss calls "a small community of quietly fanatic, changed, and truly converted Christians,"[7] and in this group we may hopefully include the pastor. Here is a group which can work as a whole, experiencing the sense of being a cell within the larger body of Christ, working quietly and effectively to open the doors to the redemptive love of God within the larger congregation. These lay people will submit to more thorough training and therefore will be more competent as teachers within the congregation. They may take over the leadership of cell-groups, the interviews with parents prior to the baptism of their children, the training of teachers in the church school, and many other such tasks, thus freeing the pastor to be the leader of leaders and pastoral director.

Within the life of the congregation, whether it is small, large or "monster," there must be opportunity for face to face personal encounter. This involves setting up small groups, numbering from twelve to twenty-five persons, who will meet together often enough to know each other as persons. They may meet in people's homes or at the Church. They do not need the leadership of the clergy, except on an overall basis, but they do need some degree of trained lay leadership, which may come from the original concerned groups we have mentioned. Such groups are not necessarily permanent; usually they are organized around both their interests and their geographical proximity to the meeting place. They may meet for Bible study, for prayer, for discussion of parental problems, for reasons of vocational interest, according to occupations, and for sociability. They must continue long enough for person-to-person encounter to develop, but they must not outlive their usefulness.

We are suggesting that the life of the local congregation is conceived normally in terms of too many people. There are certain conditions where great numbers of people can assist in

[7] John Heuss, *op. cit.*, p. 15.

witnessing to the Gospel, as at special gatherings from a number of congregations for an event representing a common achievement. Children, for example, receive a sense of belonging to a larger whole when they come together for the common presentation of a missionary offering. Our common worship is sometimes strengthened by the simple power of numbers who join in the congregational responses in a large church (and there is something of despondency in being one of a congregation of eight or ten in a building large enough for eight hundred). On occasion, special suppers and common lectures to great numbers may be beneficial. But unless one has the sense of belonging to a smaller and dynamic group, he is not likely to feel at home in a giant cathedral.

This brings up the question of the optimum size of a local congregation. It has been said that about five hundred people is as large a group as one can have for an effective ministry. If there are many more than this, the clergy cannot know the people, and if there are many less, the congregation cannot have the financial resources to support itself and give generously for the work of the Church elsewhere. Those who come from churches of this size to larger congregations often remark that it is hard to know the people in the larger parish. However, if serious attention is given to the smaller groups within the congregation, a larger parish with a multiple ministry may be as effective as the smaller parish with the limited ministry of one or two clergy. At this point, the churches could do with help from the sociologists.

Regardless of the size of the congregation, one of the most serious questions is that of the effectiveness of its worship. We have no adequate theology of worship, and those who have faced the problem often get caught either in antiquarian studies or in psychological analysis. Here it only needs to be said that a study is necessary, because it is obvious even to the untrained observer or participant that we do not have a common worship which provides an opportunity for congregational participation, liturgical reality, musical genuineness, or proclamation of the Word.

There is much more to the life of the congregation than has been mentioned here, including the relation of the parish to the homes, schools, business operations, and leisure time groups in its neighborhood. Within the educational structure of the congregation, there is a responsibility to throw the light of the Gospel on all such activities and to see their meaning within the framework of Christian faith. This points to the teaching ministry of the local congregation, as found in its worship, its fellowship, its mission, its pastoral life, its educational program, and its ecumenical relations. Even the administration of the parish, including the money-raising activities, provides opportunities for education.

In all of this certain theological demands are clear. Each individual should know himself as a child of God and an inheritor of the kingdom of God; separated from God and his fellows and under the promise of redemption through faith in Christ; experiencing the healing of those broken relationships with his fellow men and with God through the grace of the Holy Spirit; sustained in his faith and obedient to God's will as he understands it; knowing the power of God through the activities of the Church, through the proclaiming of the Word in preaching, through the sacraments, prayer, and worship, through learning God's truth and the promises of the Holy Scripture, through the pastoral care that he gives and receives, through missionary and evangelistic activities, through the acceptance of the ethical demands of the Gospel in social and personal relations, through stewardship, through membership in the total body of Christ in the ecumenical movement, and through being in the fellowship of the Holy Spirit.[8] He learns these things as he comes from the world to the Church and returns to the world.

NEW WAYS FOR THE OLD GOSPEL

It is not easy to teach an old dog new tricks. For example, in 1890, Charles Gore wrote that the Church was too much concerned with the "outward exhibition of worship," buildings and organization. "We try too much to get people to come to Church." He suggests that "it would be possible . . . to form small circles of representative men in each district, where special occupations prevail, to draw up a statement of what is wrong in current practice, and of the principles on which Christians ought to act."[9] Bishop Wickham comments that nothing happened, except among a handful of men. The Church was bound by tradition and administration to what might be called a pre-industrial

---

[8] See my *Education for Christian Living* (Englewood Cliffs: Prentice-Hall, Inc., 1956), pp. 299-300.

[9] Quoted by E. R. Wickham, *Church and People in an Industrial City*, p. 240.

way of life. There was in the Church simply no recognition of man's secular role.

There have been individual Church experiments. The problem of reaching the people in the inner city has been faced by the East Harlem Protestant Parish and those modeled after it in Cleveland and elsewhere. The clergy and their families live in the inner city, and the group ministry is developed on almost a communal basis. The effort is to reach the people where they live, and to use various aspects of the pastoral ministry to bring them into the fellowship of the Church. Store fronts are used for worship and education, due not only to lack of buildings but also to the hesitation that many people in such areas have about entering a Church building.

The people are often suspicious of a congregation shut away from the world in a special building, and this led to the house church in Halton, Leeds, England. It began with the problem of the administration of baptism, which was a meaningless service in an empty church. Attempts to bridge the gap between parents and congregation failed. So a program was worked out. When a baptism was planned, one of the clergy would visit the family. On his second visit, he would take along three or four members of the congregation. These people were among those in the congregation when the baby was baptized at a public service. This was followed up by visits based on these budding friendships, and thus the Church continued to be present in the home. This led to a new theological insight:

"The groups who had gone out to visit *for* the Church discovered that by doing so that *they* were the Church. These few people who had come to meet and talk to others in Christ's name found that they had brought the Church with them: *it was themselves.* They had gone out to discover others, and in so doing had made another discovery: that a group of Christians of *any* size, meeting to do something for Christ, can properly be called 'the Church.' . . . Being the Church to these people, they found, meant that they had to make friends with them; so one visit was not enough; further visits had to be made to let the friendship ripen."[10] However, such a lay ministry was not an easy one, and some visits were failures, but some members of the

[10] "House Church," *The Country Churchmen,* Church Album No. 6; see also Ernest Southcott, *Receive This Child* (London: Mowbrays, 1951) and *The Parish Comes Alive* (New York: Morehouse-Barlow, 1957), Gabriel Hebert, *God's Kingdom and Ours* (London: SCM Press, 1959), pp. 163-168.

congregation accepted the challenge and made it possible for this new policy on baptism to be continued. This led to careful study of the nature of the Church and of the responsibility of the laity.

As time went on, this house church idea was developed more fully. It involved groups in intensive training and prayer and in extensive house meetings carrying the love of neighbor with them. Soon Holy Communion was introduced as the proper expression of this love and devotion, and although it is not always a part of a house church meeting it is considered the normal procedure. The house church program became part of the total parish program and was extended to include a house Sunday school and a house confirmation program.

One more step was taken. In the recognition that in any housing unit there will be those of many denominations, the ecumenical house meeting was formed, to provide the opportunity for discussion of the common faith in Jesus Christ and the differences which exist between Christians. This awakening of neighbors to their common faith has made possible more effective ecumenical relations in the council of churches. Exchange of pulpits and weeks of prayer for unity have taken on new meaning.

Halton is an area of industrial housing. It is not a seriously depressed area, and the parish church is a new building beautifully situated on a hill. But instead of inviting strangers to come to church, they are invited to partake in a house church meeting with their neighbors and to share in the Lord's Supper. As a result, when they come to the parish church, their fellowship is already established and they feel that they belong with the others in the parish Eucharist.

The house church is an illustration of what one parish has done, due primarily to the untiring efforts and genius of Canon Ernest Southcott. It is not a new norm for other parishes, and yet other parishes should be challenged to find their own way of expressing vitality among the people. The Church needs a better type of organization in order to meet the demand for an effective ministry to the homes of our people, for "ordinary mortals can operate a good system, but only extraordinary ones can work effectively in a bad one."[11] In England, many theological colleges send their students to observe what is going on

[11] E. R. Wickham, *Church and People in an Industrial City,* p. 265.

in Halton, and many of the clergy are watching closely to see what permanent value this experiment may have. They are reminded of Paul's reference to Prisca and Aquila: "greet also the church in their house" (Romans 16:5, RSV).

A TEACHING CHURCH

"If education is considered as a process of growing up within the life of the group, it is immediately clear that this goes on all the time," wrote Marjorie Reeves.[12] Within the congregation we have gatherings large and small, and the members participate in both. Overall there is the pervading atmosphere of the quality of life of the total congregation. Education is going on all the time among the members. This is an inescapable fact, sometimes an unwelcome one.

This involves the local congregation in a policy of Christian education. The parish is responsible for the education of *all* of its members. The program of the church school, reaching the young up to various ages, is only a small part of the total impact of the Church on its people. *Every* organization, every activity, every worship service, and every informal meeting is part of the impact of the Christian community on its members and on others who come under its influence.

The administration needs to be set up to take account of the interpersonal relationships essential to living together as Christians. Very likely this will involve a representative group of laity who will serve as a board of Christian education for the congregation, with responsibility for a comprehensive educational program. The theological point of view is that "theology has as its complex object God in his relations to the self with its companions, and the self with its companions in their relations to God."[13] The organization of the congregation, then, must be simple and unified, for too often the local parish is so overladen with organizations that no one has time for acting as a Christian in the world. It must be flexible, in order to meet the people's needs as they arise. It must be graded, and this means being aware of the capacities of the various adults as well as of the children. It must be democratic, for only as the people

[12] Marjorie Reeves, *Growing Up in a Modern Society* (London: University of London Press, 1952), p. 11.
[13] H. Richard Niebuhr, *The Purpose of the Church and Its Ministry* (New York: Harper & Bros., 1956), p. 113.

are involved in the major decisions concerning the purposes of the Church can there be intelligent and loyal support of any program. It must be concerned with persons rather than with structure, as we saw in our study of the Church in New Testament times.[14]

Good organization and administration are essential for a sound educational program, but they do not guarantee it. Our *Church of the Immaculate Perception* runs so smoothly that nothing ever happens; and someone has said that although the Christian Church has a purpose it also gives the impression of "confusion decently and in order." Pentecost was untidy but vital. Relationships among those on the governing committees, among those charged with special tasks, among those in the cells and groups organized for individual needs, among those of all ages, determine what is happening in the parish. Good organization and administration will help the various groups from getting at cross-purposes, but something more profound is essential: an attitude pervading parish life which is open to the leading of the Holy Spirit and the redemptive love of God in Christ.

There is a certain ambiguity in the claim that the total life of the Church is educational; the same claim can be made for evangelism, missions, and fellowship. The curriculum of education is those experiences for which the Church is responsible, however, and we need to see the total picture even if our self-conscious education program is limited to specific activities.

A CLASS IS NOT A GROUP

If the local congregation is seeking to be the community of the Holy Spirit and to live as Christ's servants in the world, this will affect what goes on in classes of Christian education in the local church. Whether these classes are for younger children or older youngsters in the Church school, for parents or other adults, or for specialized meetings organized for vocational or other reasons, the same basic factors hold good.

Let us look at this class from the point of view of the teacher. It is made up of individuals who may or may not know each other, who come from a variety of backgrounds, and who have

---

[14] See Paul H. Vieth, *The Church School* (Philadelphia: Christian Education Press, 1957); also his chapter, "The Local Church Organized for Christian Education," in *Religious Education*, ed. by Marvin J. Taylor (Nashville: Abingdon Press, 1960), pp. 247-258.

individualized ways of responding to the educational situation. It is not a "group," for by this word, "group," we mean *people in a special relationship to each other.* "For where two or three are gathered in my name, there am I in the midst of them," said Jesus (Matthew 18:20, RSV).

There are strong group relationships in secular life which are similar to and yet different from the Christian fellowship. There is the "sense of the group" in many non-religiously based families, in gangs of young people which are fundamentally anti-social, on the sports field and in business concerns. Such relationships may provide resources for Christian group life, or be neutral, or be opposed.

Think of a frightened and lonely youngster who comes to a parish. He is afraid, but he covers his fear with bluster; he is alone, but he is unable to offer himself in any kind of personal encounter; he is ignorant, but he does not know what questions to ask in order to find meaning in his life. Then think of the atmosphere and organizations in the parish. There *may* be a group which can take him in, can open up his life to the grace of God whereby his fear may be cast out, his wounds may be healed, and his life may be given direction. But it is more likely that he will be invited to listen to "talks," will have an opportunity to be a spectator, will be exploited by being given a job, and will finally be lost in the crowd. He may be moved by the worship, but if there is no connection between worship and his life, even there he will be frustrated.

His needs for love and acceptance, for law and order, for direction in his growth, and for an awareness of God will not be met by any sense of "groupness," although he may often find in secular pursuits a satisfaction of these needs which he fails to find in the Church. But the Christian hope is that God will meet his needs through the community which God has set up: the Church which is the fellowship of the Holy Spirit.

The teacher looks at his class, made up of individuals who are not yet a group. It is a gathering of uncongenial minds who need to become congenial persons within the fellowship. It is ready to reflect the life of the congregation, in so far as that life is contagious and is filled with the radiance of the Gospel. The most that can be hoped for is that the class is expectant, but does not know what to expect. It is this gathering which the teacher hopes will become a Christian group. What then are the marks of a Christian group?

First, Christian group life starts with the people where they are. They have brought themselves into this gathering of fellow creatures, not always sure of their purposes but at least hopeful that they will find some worthwhile values for their lives. With them they bring certain religious convictions and hopes, combined with serious doubts and negative experiences of God and the Church. As a class and before they have become a group, the individuals provide a mixture of hopes, fears, and beliefs which need to be sorted out and evaluated.

The teacher has authority at the beginning because of his status. He is able to arrange topics and to direct the conversation. In speaking out of his own needs, he may or may not get at the needs of others in the class. What is necessary, therefore, is a technique for bringing into the open those needs of individuals in the class which can be articulated at this stage of development. What is articulated does not need to be profound, it only needs to be sincere. This is the beginning of the process whereby a class becomes a group.

Second, Christian group life starts with God. This is the other side of the coin, and less easy to understand. The members of the class have some degree of dialogue with God, and this encounter is expressed in their relationships with one another. They are aware, to some extent, of their reliance on God as their creator and sustainer. Some members of the class may be able to verbalize their faith in God and yet not to see what their relationships mean, and others may be capable of profounder interpersonal relationships without being able to verbalize them. As they become a group, they begin to comprehend (each in his own way) the Biblical story of God's mighty acts in history and their own involvement in this story.

This is not easy to understand. The task of the leader is to comprehend it for himself. We cannot expect the members of the class to have an awareness of how God works through the group, but unless the leader is aware that this is happening, he will not be able to grasp the Christian meaning of group life. This can only come from previous involvement in the life of the Christian community and from clarification through adequate leadership training.

Third, when two or more people are gathered in Christ's name, the living Lord becomes part of the encounter. This is when the presence of Christ affects the group interaction. Things happen which normally would not have happened, because God in Christ moves in a mysterious way to heal the wounds, to break down the barriers of separation, and to give sustaining power for the maintaining of fellowship no matter what strains are present.

There is no guarantee that this will happen. This is not something a teacher can manipulate. But this is what he is waiting for as he seeks to open all the doors whereby Christ may enter the lives of the members as they are together. In many classes, nothing approaching this kind of experience will occur, but it is what we wait and hope for.

Fourth, the Holy Spirit creates the kind of a group in which God's revelation may be shared. This openness to God's truth, which is at the heart of good teaching, comes through God's grace. It comes as relationships are established within the group. Reuel Howe writes, "The Holy Spirit, who brings into *being* the fellowship of love and reconciliation through that same fellowship, provides the experiences that cause us to *become reconciled* and to *be reconcilers*."[15]

Without such a group relationship, language is like the Tower of Babel, so that no one understands what others are saying. As members of the class come together and sense the meaning of their group life, they receive power from on high and a new dimension enters their lives. They may not have the words to express what is happening to them, but as they become more mature participants in the life of the group their verbal skills will increase.

Such teaching requires a sense of balance. Sara Little writes, "This means that while there will be an effort to cover content, to present a good program, to perform a task, there will also be a conscious awareness that every person is an individual of dignity and worth, capable of sharing in the making of decisions and goals, of accepting responsibility, of facing the consequences of acts, of evaluating their experiences as an aid to growth toward intellectual, spiritual, and emotional maturity."[16]

[15] Reuel L. Howe, *Man's Need and God's Action* (Greenwich: Seabury Press, 1953), p. 76; see below, pp. 85-88 for a fuller development of communication through relationships.

[16] Sara Little, *Learning Together in the Christian Fellowship* (Richmond: John Knox Press, 1956), pp. 24-25.

*What we do know is this: unless we seek to help a class to be-
come a group, nothing much of importance is going to occur.*

There are some dangers in this approach. There is a great
deal of "groupiness" which is just "buzzing" about things people
are ignorant of. Just because people talk, we do not yet have a
group. The group may become an end in itself, thus defeating
the main purpose, which is that God is the end. It may lead to
conformity, because the group as such becomes the dominant
factor in the members' lives.

There are values, however, which far outweight these dangers.
The large intellectual content of the Christian religion can best
be made relevant within the life of the group, where it becomes
possible for persons to formulate their own beliefs in their own
words. Truth is communicated primarily through persons, as we
know from the incarnation of the Word in Jesus of Nazareth, and
revelation is always in terms of experience by persons and its
interpretation. The group provides stability as the members sustain each other in their faith. Through the group sponsored by
the Church when it is truly a fellowship of the Holy Spirit, God
acts to provide the spiritual growth which is the gift of grace.[17]

There are no sure-fire methods by which a teacher can create
a group spirit. It is something that grows in a certain kind of
atmosphere, and each person has a contribution to make. This
comes in part from the existing capacity of the members to accept all the others as they are, to be forgiving and flexible and
open, to be concerned with the needs and interests of the others.
But the key person is the teacher (and in many classes the
observer also). What the leaders say and do and how they feel
and chiefly what they are become the significant factors, for these
attributes are reflected in the others, for better and for worse.
But what is even more important is the quality of life of the
congregation.

THE CONGREGATION

The basic organizational unit of Church life is the local congregation. This has always been so, even from the first days when
a congregation existed for each town visited by the apostles and
other missionaries. For here is where we find the Church in this
place. The quality of life of the congregation is directed inwardly

[17] See *ibid.,* pp. 25-29 for a similar treatment.

to the smaller groups within the congregation and affects what happens as Christians come together to form groups. It is also directed outwardly to the world around us and becomes a leaven in the immediate neighborhood and ultimately in the relations of all mankind.

But the local parish does not stand alone. Because it is the holy Catholic Church in this place, it is part of the world-wide communion of Christians, expressing this through the available organizations such as its own denominational activities throughout the world and the World Council of Churches. As the class becomes a group, it becomes aware of the larger fellowship, and in a sense this larger fellowship indwells the group. "I believe in the holy Catholic Church in this place."

CHAPTER VI

Communication Within the Church

THE Church's task is to communicate the Gospel. We can see this as a primary effort in the New Testament Church. To communicate is to transmit to people "what one intensely believes and feels, in order to interest, persuade, convince, and move," says W. Russell Bowie.[1] Or as Father Delcuve puts it, its aim "is to work with grace in the awakening or the increase of that faith which justifies us."[2] This is the kind of communication we see in the New Testament reports of the preaching of Peter; it is what we see in the impact of Philip; it is the effect of the preaching and the letters of Paul. And in every case, it is communication from adults to adults.

The New Testament has a good deal to say about the significance of children, but practically nothing to provide guidance for training. Children are included in the fellowship because of their relationship with their parents, and it is up to the parents to provide the training. In relation to infant baptism in the next century, as Father Sloyan reports, "all the evidence available (or better the lack of it) indicates that it was left to Christian parents and godparents to instruct their offspring in the truths of the faith. No treatise directed to parents or children exists."[3]

The starting point of communication is to have something worth sharing. Because we believe with intensity that God revealed himself in Jesus Christ, we have no choice but to share the good news. Because we believe that this news is dynamic, we are enabled by God's grace to sow seeds of faith in others. Something

[1] W. Russell Bowie, *Preaching* (Nashville: Abingdon Press, 1958), p. 13.

[2] George Delcuve, in *Shaping the Christian Message,* ed. by Gerard S. Sloyan (New York: Macmillan & Co., 1958), p. 281.

[3] Gerard S. Sloyan in *ibid.,* p. 17; see William Barclay, *Train Up a Child: Educational Ideals in the Ancient World* (Philadelphia: Westminster Press, 1959), pp. 234-236.

unique and incomparable happened in the succession of instances which we call the "event" of Jesus Christ, for in the life, death, and resurrection of Jesus Christ and in the coming of the Church as founded on him, we can see revealed both the utterly destructive power of human sin and the saving love of God; this is something which happened in human history and can be dated, but it is also something which is repeated in human experience every moment of our existence. The communication of this message can never be something as dry as dust, it can never be an archeological expedition into the past, it can never be the accumulation of information. It is a message with an explosive idea, powerful enough to release the hidden powers of God in our lives.

The first danger in communication is that there may be no news to disseminate. Like the speeches attributed to President Harding, what we say may be "an army of pompous phrases, moving over the landscape in search of an idea."[4] But even when we are overwhelmed by the power of the Christian message, there can be no communication unless there is personal encounter. Two stories are told of Martin Buber. At the end of a long discussion, a man said to him, "You are right." Buber was dismayed, for this meant that he had won the man to the God of the philosophers rather than to a living Person to whom one says "Thou." And he commented, "I could only return his gaze." This can be contrasted with a similar situation in which there was no agreement. But at the end, Buber reports, "the old man stood up, came over to me, laid his hands on my shoulder, and spoke: 'Let us be friends.' The conversation was completed. For where two or three are truly together, they are together in the name of God."[5]

It is this response of a person to a person which is essential to genuine communication. It is within the community that one responds meaningfully to what is said. The content may be in the form of relationships, words, or things, but the important point is that those taking part in the personal encounter can say, "God

[4] Halford Luccock, *Communicating the Gospel* (New York: Harper & Bros., 1953), p. 82.
[5] Quoted in *Religious Education*, (Jan.-Feb. 1959) 54:6-7, by Maurice Friedman from Martin Buber, *Eclipse of God: Studies in the Relation between Religion and Philosophy* (New York: Harper & Bros., 1957), pp. 3-9.

himself is with us." Communication is the appropriation of a revelation.

H. Richard Niebuhr defines revelation in our history to "mean that special occasion which provides us with an image by means of which all the occasions of personal and common life become intelligible."[6] If this is so, then Lewis J. Sherrill is right in claiming that Christian education "is concerned with the meeting between God and the human creature, and with the tension which rises within the encounter, calling for human response to God and divine response to man."[7] Communication, education, and evangelism are equally the activity of the Holy Spirit when seen against the background of this interpretation of revelation. This is the kind of encounter we hope to find within the Christian community.

Communication takes place within a community, but we must remember also that the community educates. A family educates its children by the kind of family life they experience together. A school educates through the morale and moral quality of life. The marks of the community rub off on all its members, and it is within this atmosphere that everything is heard and interpreted. Do all the members recognize themselves as subject to the rule of law? Do all members treat each other as persons? Does each member find a significant part to play and see the purpose of his participation? Is there some purpose greater than self-interest at the center of the group's loyalty? Is there enough mixture of interest and personality to make genuine tensions and differences certain to occur?[8] As Marjorie Reeves says, no matter how elaborate a program we may have for our youth work, for example, "the general body of church members must never forget that they are ultimately responsible for the education of the youth in their midst. They must continually ask themselves: 'Are we the kind of church that shows forth in its life the truth of God?' "[9]

The basis of Christian communication is always this person-to-person encounter. "The best way to send an idea," said Robert Oppenheimer, "is to wrap it up in a person."[10] This is a neat

---

[6] H. Richard Niebuhr, *The Meaning of Revelation* (New York: Macmillan & Co., 1941) , p. 109; see above, pp. 34-35.

[7] Lewis J. Sherrill, *The Gift of Power* (New York: Macmillan & Co.), p. 90.

[8] See Marjorie Reeves, *Growing Up in a Modern Society*, p. 35.

[9] *Ibid.*, p. 82.

[10] Quoted by Halford Luccock, *Communicating the Gospel*, p. 100.

definition of one aspect of the incarnation, for when we say that "the Word became flesh and dwelt among us," we are asserting that God's revelation of himself took place in a person, and that this is the center of our faith.

THE LANGUAGE OF RELATIONSHIPS

The most exciting phrase in Christian education today is Reuel Howe's "the language of relationships."[11] In another context it may be referred to as "relationship theology" or the "theology of relationships." It presents communication as the result of genuine encounter between persons, rather than as an exchange of words. It does not have to be non-verbal, but words are never the basic element in what occurs.

Howe tells the story of a timid teacher who has in her class a sullen fourteen year old boy named Joe. He made life miserable for her and she became more and more afraid, and finally she kept him after school and asked him why he was picking on her. "For a moment he looked sullenly at her and then replied, 'Because you're such a sucker for it.'

" 'I know I am,' she sighed. 'I've always been afraid of people like you, and yet I'd like to help you. Isn't there some other reason why you're always fighting and picking on people who can't take care of themselves? Don't you want anyone to love you and help you?' "

In a moment she had a crying boy to confront, and he told her his sordid story of rejection and anxiety which lay behind his bullying. "Her honesty as a person called forth the truth from this confused and resentful boy. . . . Having experienced the power of the personal from one who as a person did not seem to have much power, he was set on his way, through her, to becoming a person. On the other hand, her strength, to no small degree, rested in her ability to be honest about her timidity. And that honesty reached him so that he knew she accepted him, his anxiety about himself, and his hostility toward her. In other words, her power to accept herself became her power to accept him, and this made it possible for him in turn to accept himself. This is what we mean by the power of the personal: *The power to help one another to become and remain persons.*"[12]

The teacher needs this kind of insight in order to communi-

[11] Reuel Howe, *Man's Need and God's Action*, p. 75.

[12] Reuel Howe, *The Creative Years* (Greenwich: Seabury Press, 1959), pp. 21-22.

cate anything at all, but it takes humility to admit that he can do nothing more than accept the pupil as he is and to admit that the pupil probably regards him as an authority-figure, or even as an object of scorn. The starting point of Christian education is this seeking to create an atmosphere in which the pupil is able to recognize the fact that he is accepted as a person. Then comes a feeling of confidence on the pupil's part and resistance is overcome. He accepts his teacher as a person; he trusts the teacher because the teacher is taking part in his life, accepting him before seeking to influence him. Then the pupil learns to ask questions because he trusts his teacher as a person. The impersonal "I-it" relationship has been overcome by the "I-thou" relationship.[13]

"This," says Howe, "is what I call the language of relationship, the communication that results from living together and which gives us the basic and personal meanings for the words we hear and use. The spirit of the relationships determines the nature of the communication."[14] This description is obvious in the understanding we have of infancy when words are not possible. We know that communication takes place, and we rejoice in our memories of the personal contact and encounter between parents and little children. What we do not realize is that this same kind of personal relationship is essential to any communication in the future, no matter how much we can rely also on words, symbols, and things.

This insight is crucial for understanding the key words of Christian living. *Faith* is the description of a personal relationship; it is an attitude of trust in the living God, of commitment to him as he appears in our lives either in direct experience or through the experience of other persons. Faith is not something fundamentally intellectual; its vitality lies in the fact that it is interpersonal and relational. It issues in renewed attitudes and in action. Faith may improve our understanding by its new perspective, but it is not in itself an organ of knowledge.

Love is relational and exists between persons. It is also an attitude: It "is patient and kind; love is not jealous or boastful; it is not arrogant or rude. Love does not insist on its own way; it is not irritable or resentful; it does not rejoice at wrong, but re-

[13] See my *Be Not Anxious*, pp. 66-67; see also Martin Buber, *Between Man and Man* (London: Routledge & Kegan Paul, 1947), pp. 83-117, for a full treatment of this idea.

[14] *Man's Need and God's Action*, p. 75.

joices in the right. Love bears all things, believes all things, endures all things. Love never ends" (I Corinthians 13:4-8, RSV).

Hope also involves personal relationships. "Hope always means waiting for something we haven't yet got. But if we hope for something we cannot see, then we must settle down to wait for it in patience" (Romans 8:24-25, P). "The Christian Church is a community of hopeful believers," writes Reinhold Niebuhr.[15] It anticipates a fuller relationship with God, because of the promise of eternal life.

The process of *reconciliation* and *forgiveness,* offered to us by the free *grace* of God, is a description of a new relationship, experienced in the community of the Holy Spirit. "For if while we were enemies we were reconciled to God by the death of his Son, much more, now that we are reconciled, shall we be saved by his life. Not only so, but we also rejoice in God through our Lord Jesus Christ, through whom we have now received reconciliation" (Romans 5:10-11, RSV).

These relationships are evident in the Christian home, where we learn to listen to one another because we are responsible for one another and serve one another, but unless we already accept one another, we cannot listen or serve with any degree of adequacy. As Horace Bushnell put it, "And it must be first, not in words or talk, but visibly first in your love—that which fixes your aims, feeds your enjoyments, sanctifies your pleasures, supports your trials, satisfies your wants, contents your ambitions, beautifies and blesses your character. No mock piety, no sanctimony of phrase, no longitude of face on Sundays will suffice. You must live in the light of God, and hold such a spirit in exercise as you wish to see translated into your children. You must take them into your feeling, as a loving and joyous element, and beget, if by the grace of God you may, the spirit of your own heart in theirs."[16]

This problem of communication through the language of relationships permeates the whole of our society. The sickness in our race relations is precisely here. What is wanted by the Negro is acceptance as a person. He "doesn't seek integration because he wants to be among whites, but because he wants to be

---

[15] Reinhold Niebuhr, *Faith and History* (New York: Charles Scribner's Sons, 1949), p. 238.
[16] Horace Bushnell, *Christian Nurture,* p. 45.

treated like a man. . . . If freedom and human dignity are lacking, the fact that the Negro may be content, indifferent, or well cared for has little to do with the real problem."[17]

The danger is that the Church or society will seek to solve these problems of communication through relationships on a purely secular or human plane. The doctrine of the Holy Spirit, with its emphasis on the immanence of God, may give rise to a corporate mysticism but may lose sight of God's transcendence. Man's ultimate relation is always to God, and God stands over against man as the Creator over the creature. It is this dual relationship which makes man what he is. It gives him a perspective on this world as God's world and yet as only one world among others. "At one and the same time," says Joseph Sittler, "it relativizes all things human and historical, and makes the human decision and the historical behavior absolutely crucial."[18] It keeps him from making an idol of the cause of justice and decency, and yet it makes his will to justice and decency essential to the meaning of his life. He learns to see God at work beneath the surface of human events without identifying God with the event. But without the language of relationships, he would have no experience by which to point to God at all. That is why an incarnation was necessary, for his faith centers on the historical event by which "in Christ God was reconciling the world to himself" (II Corinthians 5:19).

THE LANGUAGE OF WORDS

Paul said, "Lo! I tell you a mystery" (I Corinthians 15:51, RSV). We are to proclaim "the mystery of the gospel" (Ephesians 6:19, RSV). We hear of "the mystery of Christ" (Ephesians 3:4, RSV). It is proclaimed and told and shown, but it is not explained. This is the basic difficulty with religious language. It becomes foolishness to the Greeks when they submit it to their logical analysis and a stumbling block to the Jews when they test it by their own history. Yet Ian T. Ramsey declares that only through adequate analysis of the logical structure of religious language can we learn how to use it effectively. Religious language seeks to evoke a special discernment of reality which will lead to total commitment. "No one has ever seen God"

[17] Louis J. Twomey, in *What Is the Nature of Man?* (Philadelphia: Christian Education Press, 1959), p. 199.
[18] Joseph Sittler, in *ibid.*, p. 189.

(John 1:18, RSV), and yet only by discerning the presence of God can there be evoked a response that amounts to faith or commitment.

Religious language deals with "characteristically personal situations," which means that it cannot use the objective and impersonal descriptions of even the social sciences, which might describe the processes of a court of justice, but must describe what is unique. It discerns something deeper than what appears on the surface; it provides a "new dimension" in which the light suddenly dawns; it is like a bit of humor that breaks the ice at a party; it gets through to the personal.

Religious language also deals with commitment. Ramsey shows how a mathematician makes commitments to certain formulas in order to solve a problem, or a sportsman to his game, or a lover to his lass. Religious commitment, he suggests, includes the breadth of a mathematical commitment and the depth of personal loyalty.

In order to achieve these ends of discernment and commitment, religious language has taken on certain odd uses. The name, God, is personal and yet it has no distinctive meaning. God tells Moses simply that "I am I," and the Jews avoid using the term "Yahweh" and substitute "The Lord." This is the logic of "nicknames," where the object is clear only to those who discern him. Even straightforward words take on new meanings and are sometimes transformed. There are certain key words which evoke a response by those who believe. Odd devices are used, with quotation marks, hyphens, and capital letters applied to normal words. Words are mixed in strange fashions. Tautologies are used, such as "Duty for duty's sake," "Conscience is conscience," "Duty is God's will," "Conscience is God's voice," "God is Love."

Ramsey uses many more illustrations to make his points. Religious language, he tells us, is "logically odd." It is based on a discernment which is "perceptual and more," and therefore the situation becomes different, and he describes this as "the light dawning, the ice breaking, the penny dropping." When this happens, we may yield to the reality behind the new insight with a total commitment.

This leads first to a negative warning: "Let us always be cautious of talking about God in straightforward language. Let us never talk as if we had privileged access to the diaries of God's private life, or expert insight into his descriptive psychology, so that we say quite cheerfully why God did what, when, and where."[19]

At no point is Ramsey suggesting that because religious language has a certain oddity that it speaks nonsense. On the contrary, it is dealing with the personal on a deeper level than is possible with straightforward descriptions.

Another way of stating this is to say that religious language is the language of revelation, and its purpose is to evoke a response of wonder and worship. This cannot be accomplished by a matter-of-fact description. At the same time, the words are concrete, what Father Divine calls "tangibilizing." They are active and dramatic words. Ramsey uses the example of "Son of Man." This term, he suggests, as used by Jesus, had no clear theological meaning, and although it *could* refer to Jesus it was not clear that Jesus meant it that way. The final disclosure that Jesus was this Son of Man came only after the resurrection. They had called him "Messiah," but the thought of a crucified Messiah was impossible. They had heard that the Son of Man would be killed and rise again. So "when the light dawned and the penny dropped, 'Messiah' had to become 'crucified and risen Messiah'—a logical impropriety indeed—before it could even claim to be appropriate currency for a phrase equivalent to 'Son of Man,' whose full significance was now, and for the first time, seen. So significant indeed was this phrase that it was rarely used again. For it had proved to be a phrase used by Jesus to name himself."[20]

Ramsey also refers to the sermon of Peter at Pentecost with its "riotous mixture of phrases," which "is in effect a rough and ready attempt to secure that special logical impropriety needed to express the Christian message. Each word is logically qualified by the presence of the others, and in this way each word comes to display a suitable measure of impropriety." He illustrates this with the following italicized words: "God hath glorified his *servant (child)* Jesus whom ye delivered up. . . . Ye denied *the Holy* and *the Righteous One* . . . and killed the *Prince (Author) of Life* whom God raised from the dead." (Acts 3:13, 14, 15) . "God hath made him *both Lord* and *Christ,* this

[19] Ian T. Ramsey, *Religious Language* (London: SCM Press, 1957), p. 91; see pp. 11-48.
[20] Ian T. Ramsey, *ibid.*, p. 143.

Jesus whom ye crucified" (Acts 2:36) . This was the primitive proclamation, and it was effective because it evoked a response to a situation which could be discerned only if the language were sufficiently odd.

Ramsey offers one other example which is pertinent, especially in view of what we have said about the significance of community and the language of relationships. It is often claimed that the resurrection has its best evidence in the existence of the Church, and Ramsey says that "the logical moves in this claim are two: (1) the Church is offered as something which evokes or expresses Christian commitment; (2) this commitment is then brought to the Resurrection narratives. . . . The important practical point is that it is no use telling people that the Church is the best evidence for the Resurrection unless already . . . the Church evokes in them the kind of situation which must always be the empirical anchorage for a significant theology."[21]

Another way of approaching this problem of the words of the Christian faith is suggested by Canon F. H. Drinkwater, who says that we must use "the language of the heart." There is a language which seals off the heart, like a fuse-box, and this may be necessary for repairs, but we don't expect light or heat during these circumstances. He says there are four classes of language: scientific-difficult, such as the language of Einstein or Thomas Aquinas; scientific-simple, such as a weather forecast or a business letter; poetic-difficult, such as Francis Thompson's "The Hound of Heaven;" and poetic-simple, such as Lincoln's Gettysburg Address. Whenever a poet gets to the heart, he uses simple words:

> "Good night, sweet prince,
> And flights of angels sing thee to thy rest!"[22]

He is not deriding theology which uses technical terms. He is aware of the fact that theology "must erect a lofty structure of truth expressed in scientific language upon a basis of truth expressed in non-scientific language. It is like building a mighty bridge not on solid ground but across some wide river bed.

[21] Ian T. Ramsey, *ibid.*, p. 131.
[22] F. H. Drinkwater, in *Shaping the Religious Message,* ed. by Gerard S. Sloyan, pp. 274-275.

This can be done to last, but not by any second-rate engineers in a hurry."[23]

Communication through words goes astray when teachers try to translate the scientific-difficult into scientific-simple, for we have to go a step further and translate it into poetic-simple. In the words of Yeats:

> "God guard me from the thoughts men think
> In the mind alone.
> He that sings a lasting song
> Thinks in a marrow bone."[24]

The response to religious discernment is wonder, amazement, enthrallment, enthusiasm. It is found primarily in the atmosphere of worship.

Not for a moment does this discount the significance of Biblical scholarship, historical accuracy, or theological technicalities. But it places religious language in its proper religious dimension for purposes of communication when the goal is nurture and commitment based on discernment. When the teacher is asked, "Did Jesus live?" the answer should be in matter-of-fact language suitable to the questioner; but when the question is, "Who was Jesus?" the answer should be in terms of poetic-simple language, for now there is the desire for discernment and commitment.

Story telling becomes perhaps the most important of all forms of teaching. Certainly the parable was significant in the mind of Jesus himself. At the end of the parable there would be a question, and, in Ramsey's terms, "the light dawned, the penny dropped." Our best stories are often thinly disguised parables, based on the stories Jesus told but in a modern and relevant setting. The Bible as a whole is seen as a story, a drama, and therefore it is possible to keep the whole Bible in proper perspective. This is why "lives of Jesus"[25] are consistently popular. The early preaching in Acts, with all of its riotous mixing of

[23] F. H. Drinkwater, in *ibid.*, p. 277.

[24] Quoted by Luccock, *Communicating the Gospel*, p. 37.

[25] For juniors see Norman Langford, *The King Nobody Wanted* (Philadelphia: Westminster Press, 1948); for seniors and adults, see my *I Remember Jesus* (Greenwich: Seabury Press, 1958) and John Knox, *The Man Christ Jesus* (New York: Harper & Bros., 1941). Notice the possibility of discernment and commitment in reading these books.

metaphors and phrases, was a recounting of what had happened to Jesus and through Jesus. This is image-thinking, story-thinking, drama-thinking.

Poetry itself becomes important. One of the most moving of modern religious poets was Studdert-Kennedy, whose verses were not always great poetry but who always told a story that led toward discernment and commitment. Take, for example, this story:

> "And, sitting down, they watched Him there,
> The soldiers did;
> There, while they played with dice,
> He made His sacrifice,
> And died upon the Cross to rid
> God's world of sin.
> He was a gambler, too, my Christ,
> He took His life and threw
> It for a world redeemed.
> And ere His agony was done,
> Before the westering sun went down,
> Crowning that day with its crimson crown,
> He knew that He had won."[26]

This emphasis on the poetic-simple in language is not an appeal for a "simple Gospel." When we reduce the message to scientific-simple, we often get a watered down picture of Christianity, but by the use of the poetic-simple we are able to get to the basic elements of the faith. Phillips Brooks, in his *Lectures on Preaching*, said, "Never be afraid to bring the transcendent mysteries of our faith, Christ's death and resurrection, to the help of the humblest and commonest of human wants. There is a sort of preaching which keeps them for the great emergencies, and soothes the common sorrows and rebukes the common sins with lower considerations of economy. Such preaching fails. It is useful neither as a law nor as a gospel. It neither appeals to the lower nor the higher perceptions of mankind. It is like a river that is frozen too hard to be navigated but not hard enough to bear. Never fear, as you preach, to bring the sublimest motive to the smallest duty, and the most infinite comfort to

[26] G. A. Studdert-Kennedy, *The Unutterable Beauty* (London: Hodder & Stoughton, 1927), p. 117. Some of his poetry is included with some other writings in *The Best of Studdert-Kennedy* (New York: Harper & Bros., 1948).

the smallest trouble. They will prove they belong there, if only the duty and trouble are real, and you have read them thoroughly aright."[27]

The Christian faith is made up of great words, mostly of one syllable. When a person using these words is mastered by a supreme conviction and is concerned with the "I-thou" relationship, these words can reach the heart. The poetic-simple points to the mystery, and even the scientific-difficult can do no more, for no one can explain the mystery. The great themes speak to the simplest wants.

In the use of words for communication, there needs to be the opportunity for genuine dialogue. The repetition in parrot-like fashion of memorized phrases has doubtful value, unless there is the opportunity also to rephrase what has been said in one's own words. There is always the danger that people will be made passive through words, for they may be "interested only in the gentle inward message that the sounds of words give them," says S. I. Hayakawa. "Just as cats and dogs like to be stroked, so do some human beings like to be verbally stroked at fairly regular intervals."[28] There is never any certainty that this passivity can be avoided, but through discussion, use of observers, "feed-back," use of tape recorders, and other techniques, it is possible to determine the extent to which there is confrontation with the realities of the faith in the teaching situation.

THE LANGUAGE OF THINGS

Genuine Christian communication is always a two-way proposition within the community. It builds on relationships, uses words to express the fundamental reality of relationships with God and man, and often finds that things are a means of discourse. Symbols may be words or things. As words, we are aware that symbols stand for something or suggest something, perhaps vaguely, or simply create an atmosphere or an emotional response. But symbols are also pictures, statues, or forms which carry meaning. Symbols can be things as well as words.

Symbols are the means whereby something is made intelligible or accessible. They point beyond themselves and share in the reality of that to which they point. Signs merely point to

[27] Phillips Brooks, *Lectures on Preaching* (New York: E. P. Dutton, 1877), pp. 27-28.
[28] Quoted in Luccock, *Communicating the Gospel*, p. 133.

something, writes Paul Tillich, but symbols actually participate in the power of that which they symbolize.[29] They "open up levels of reality which are otherwise closed to us."[30] "Nobody can invent or abolish them."[31]

The significance of symbols is that they are able to point beyond what can be grasped by the senses or the rational mind, they represent what cannot be communicated in non-symbolic terms, they are drawn from the common life, they are directly or indirectly related to that to which they point, and they are concrete.[32] Yet symbols are never identical with what they refer to, even though they participate in some degree in the reality to which they point.[33]

F.W. Dillistone writes, "Man's supreme need at the present time is to become related to powerful and meaningful symbols. They must be such as to integrate him into the *wholeness* of the natural environment to which he belongs: such as to bind him to his fellow-men by ties which are deeply *personal*. They must on the one hand be flexible enough to allow for an expanding knowledge of the universe; they must, on the other hand, be of such a pattern as to make room for a continuing dialectic between man and man."[34]

Certain symbols maintain their power to make persons whole and to communicate truth because they are deeply grounded in nature, but to the man who has turned his back on nature such symbols may cease to be valuable, and therefore he must either find new symbols or lose his rootage in reality. Because symbols operate at both the conscious and unconscious level, they need either to be retained or replaced, for man cannot live without them.

One of the earliest Christian symbols was the fish. The word was an acrostic, based on the Greek I-CH-TH-U-S, the letters standing for "Jesus Christ, Son of God and Savior." Cyril C. Richardson suggests that the symbol became significant be-

---

[29] Paul Tillich, in *Religious Symbolism*, ed. by F. Ernest Johnson (New York: Harper & Bros., 1955), p. 109.

[30] Paul Tillich, *Dynamics of Faith* (New York: Harper & Bros., 1957), p. 42.

[31] In *Religious Symbolism*, p. 109.

[32] I am aware that mathematical and some poetic symbols are abstract, and usually meaningless to the layman.

[33] See Lewis J. Sherrill, *The Gift of Power*, pp. 124-125.

[34] F. W. Dillistone, *Christianity and Symbolism* (London: Collins, 1955), p. 296.

cause of the origin of Christianity among fishermen; to them the fish was something mysterious, associated with holy food. In the Fourth Gospel, a fish was used sacramentally by the risen Lord (John 21:9-14). The acrostic was possibly an afterthought. The symbol has a variety of meanings: Christ as the fisherman, fish as eucharistic food, fish as the sign of Jonah, and dolphin as the friend of man.[35] It seems to have come back into favor, although perhaps accidentally, in churches designed as fish. It is not likely to have universal acceptance as a central Christian symbol, although it may have value as a peripheral one.

Dillistone suggests that baptism may have a deeper significance than some other symbolic acts, because water does not lose its connection with washing in an industrial society. Water shortages are as vivid to the city-dweller as to the farmer. The baptismal liturgy should be very simple. "Nothing is essential save the symbolic initiation *through water* into the organism of the Triune God—Father, Son and Holy Spirit—who creates and sustains and purifies and enhances the life of the whole universe."[36] Water is seen as sacramental, and a dramatic action is performed with it. Dillistone questions whether this act is sufficiently meaningful by itself in the urban and industrial areas. He suggests that the registration of one's name is the most widely used form of commitment, and that this "commitment-into-the-Name-ritual" when associated with baptism may help us to maintain the significance of the symbolism of both water and naming.

The symbolism of bread and wine, while still meaningful in rural areas, says Dillistone, can be effective in urban areas only in terms of the experience of personal relationships. Not the blood symbol but the common sharing is what is important, provided it is seen in terms of both communion and commitment.[37]

The symbol which has the greatest possibility of remaining significant is the cross, for it is grounded in history and tells a story. An empty cross speaks of both the crucifixion and resurrection and therefore points to the victory over both the death of sin and physical death. Among those Protestants who have been suspicious of symbols, the use of the cross as a meaningful symbol has increased.

[35] See Cyril C. Richardson, in *Religious Symbolism*, ed. by F. Ernest Johnson, pp. 5-8.
[36] F. W. Dillistone, *Christianity and Symbolism*, p. 297.
[37] See *ibid.*, pp. 296-303.

When Christian symbols lose their power, two things are likely to happen. First, new symbols are drawn from secular life and often they cannot be tied in with the historical meaning of Christianity. Halford Luccock writes that Mother's Day is the high point of the Church year in Middletown: "Middletown believes in mothers. The symbol of that type of religion becomes not a cross but a carnation."[38] Second, we find a religious faith barren of all symbolism, and therefore religion loses its power. H. Richard Niebuhr's characterization of modern religion shows what can happen: "A God without wrath brought men without sin into a kingdom without judgment through the ministrations of a Christ without a cross."[39]

The twentieth-century man has difficulty with symbols. All he sees is a stained glass window which he cannot understand, or a series of picture-words which seem unrelated to his life. He does not see the potentiality of the symbol, which, says Sherrill, "sets the mind soaring out into an unbounded area, stimulates the mind to do its own work of recognizing the meaning in the symbol, and encourages the quest for further meaning."[40] Symbols are to be understood with something of the logical impropriety we saw to be present in religious language. They cause puzzlement to the inquiring mind, and this forces the believer to seek for deeper meanings.

Sherrill lists the different kinds of symbols to be found in the Bible: objects such as blood and wine, forces of nature, persons playing roles, ritualized actions, names, miracle stories, visions, and others.[41] It is not always clear how these symbols were used or are to be used, and we need to remember that symbols grow and then die, and that they do not necessarily have the same meanings for successive generations. There is much in Biblical imagery which is nonsense to the twentieth-century man, and even the explanations of modern scholars are not always helpful.

If one visits the cathedrals of Europe, he will find an ornate cathedral in Rome or Munich, a much simpler Lutheran cathedral (which once was ornate) in Berlin, and a cathedral bare of almost all symbolism in Geneva. The outward archi-

---

[38] Halford E. Luccock, *Communicating the Gospel*, p. 162.

[39] H. Richard Niebuhr, *The Kingdom of God in America* (New Haven: The Shoe String Press, 1954), p. 193.

[40] Lewis J. Sherrill, *The Gift of Power*, p. 126.

[41] See *ibid.*, pp. 128-144.

tecture in each case may be Gothic or Norman or Renaissance, but the symbolism on the interior points to the reality of God in different ways. Today, as new churches are being designed, we discover a move away from the New England meeting house to the church "in the round" or the modern church in the shape of a fish or the other creative expressions utilizing modern insights. Within all these churches, certain symbols recur with regularity: the Lord's Table, pulpit and lectern, the Bible on the table or lectern, the font, the windows and frescoes or other forms of art. The worship in these churches makes use of certain liturgical practices and words, the sermon is preached, the sacraments are administered. There are experiments with new forms, new music, and even a "folk mass." The members of the congregation respond vocally and also with such symbolic acts as sitting, standing and kneeling. Always before them is the central Christian symbol of the cross, and always there is some expression of the Church's vision of its outreach to the whole world. Often we belong to the congregation on the basis of the meaningfulness of its symbols.

The difficulty is that symbols are not always universal. They have meaning only within a worshiping congregation which has learned to use them. It is difficult to bring back to life those symbols which are forgotten, such as the yoke, or to create new symbols for today. The inner dynamics of meaningful symbols needs further study. The Friends, in rejecting the traditional symbols, have the symbolism of the handshake between leaders to close their silent meeting; some Protestants think that genuflection and the sign of the cross of their Catholic brethren, especially when performed before images, to be a form of idolatry.

Both verbal and non-verbal symbols are limited to the community in which they have been found useful, and within such a community non-verbal symbols perform functions which verbal symbols cannot perform. Within such a community, they are the means of growth in grace as they become expressions of increased discernment and commitment. In this way, new symbols do arise as the expression of the congregation's yearning, and their possibility of being universal depends on their capacity to interpret the common life of the age. For example, Gabriel Hebert tells of a new book on the passion and resurrection of Christ which contains illustrations from every-day life. "If we want to live through and feel what Christ lived through and felt, let us look around us and see pictures taken from our own life, which will show us what Christ lived through and suffered." There follows a series of photographs of life in Paris: pictures from a newspaper or a news-magazine, from a family album, from the street, showing people in their relationships to each other. It is in this environment that we need to see the reality of God at work.[42]

In order for symbols to be meaningful, we need a three-point program. First, children need to be exposed to those traditional symbols which retain their meaning. During the period when picture language is easily grasped, much can be done to interpret the meanings of the simpler and more obvious symbols. Second, each congregation tends to develop its own symbolism which it shares with the tradition in which it stands. At first, this will lead to a self-consciousness concerning the use and meanings of the symbols available in the worship and architecture of the Church, but it should lead on to the third point, which is experimentation in the use of new symbols. Congregations which build new churches have a special obligation, it seems to me, to seek for new symbols and for radical uses of old ones. Careful study of architecture and liturgical practices will be necessary, and this may lead to valuable insights even if the final decisions follow more traditional lines. Exploration of new uses for the "language of things" should be an on-going process in every congregation.

THE RELIGIOUS DIMENSION

Such communication through relationships, words, and symbols is not easy. "After all," wrote Horace Bushnell, "there is no cheap way of making Christians of our children. Nothing but practically to live it makes it sure."[43] The religious dimension of life is the primary orientation of Christian communication. We are seeking always to make possible an increasing discernment of the presence of God within the community and an increasing commitment to God's will in our daily lives. This kind of communication goes on in the Church's worship, fellowship, mission, pastoral care, ecumenical relations, and specific instruction, and to these functions and their educational implications we turn in Part II of this book.

[42] See Gabriel Hebert, *God's Kingdom and Ours*, pp. 161-162.
[43] Horace Bushnell, *Christian Nurture*, p. 72.

Part II

CHAPTER VII

A Worshiping Congregation

WORSHIP stands at the center of all religion. It is not something peculiar to Christianity but is an expression of the yearning of all mankind for communion with the divine. It is a corporate act by the congregation, Christian or Jewish, Moslem or Hindu or Buddhist. The background of Christian worship is the practice of the Jewish synagogue. It was Jesus' custom to attend the synagogue on the sabbath day; on one occasion he read from Isaiah and interpreted what he had read in a manner offensive to his fellow townsmen. The service contained psalms, common prayer and confession of faith, reading from the law and the prophets, and preaching. At first, the early Christians worshipped with the Jews in the synagogues, but in time they were thrown out because of their "heresy," and they set up their own service on the same model. This type continued as a form of worship separate from the Lord's Supper for at least four centuries, and continues today in Protestantism as the non-sacramental worship which precedes or exists independently of the Lord's Supper.

Worship always has been a form of service. Although modeled after the synagogue, variations soon crept into the customs of these early Christians as they worshiped in open spaces, in homes, and wherever else they were free to gather. They followed Paul's instruction: "Let the word of Christ dwell in you richly, as you teach and admonish one another in all wisdom, and as you sing psalms and hymns and spiritual songs with thankfulness in your hearts to God. And whatever you do, in word or deed, do everything in the name of the Lord Jesus, giving thanks to God the Father through him" (Colossians 3:16-17, RSV).

Worship is the congregation's conscious relationship with God. A new dimension of life confronts them as they accept their place in the covenant relationship established by Christ and as they see that God is working out his purpose in history and in their own lives. They seek the Lord and then stand in awe before him. They feel dependent on the holy God who transcends all creation and yet is immanent in the processes of their daily lives. This sense of the presence of a cosmic reality restores the worshipers to their proper place in the universe, acknowledges their creaturehood and yet asserts that they belong to a cosmic God. They affirm the "worth-ship" of God.

Bernard E. Meland described worship as "the *lunge toward reality.* It is the conscious effort to throw off the sham, the superficial, the trivial and sordid crustations that gather about us in daily associations. Without this effort we tend to become calloused by social niceties and poses, which, perhaps, are necessary concessions to the folkways of our environs, but invariably pernicious when not countered by a shrug of the shoulders or a vigorous effort to stand upright and attentive before standards and values that are objective and actual and before which we dare make no concessions."[1]

In worship, we come before the Lord as a corporate body of sinners needing repentance, as believers who know that because Christ died for us forgiveness is possible, as listeners to the Word of God revealed in the mighty acts of God recorded in the Bible and interpreted in the sermon, as men of faith who affirm that faith, as those who know the real presence of Christ in the Lord's Supper, as those who offer their own petitions to the Lord in terms of "not my will, but thine, be done," and as those assured of the blessing of God upon us all.

The wonder of worship is that God is present. In our praise, it is God who is praised. In our confession, it is God who hears and forgives. In our listening, it is God whom we hear. In our speaking, it is God who listens. In our symbolic formulas, it is God who is represented.

The casual worshiper and the outsider do not always recog-

[1] Bernard E. Meland, *Modern Man's Worship* (New York: Harper & Bros., 1934), p. 228.

nize God at work through our worship. They observe the congregation from an outside vantage point, and therefore they are not in a position to evaluate the process that takes place in worship. They have no way of sensing the redemptive and healing and sustaining powers that are given to the worshipers through their encounter with God. Their only test is a practical one: "Are these people any better for having worshiped?" Often their conclusion is negative and accurate: "There is no difference in them discernible to the eye. Nothing has happened in worship; therefore, the Church is no good."

The honest worshiper often comes to the same conclusion, both about himself and about others. Nothing has happened. Sin has not been eradicated. What God has done in Christ is not evident. The process of salvation seems to have been short-circuited. This may be due to the failure of the Church truly to worship, but more often it lies in the unwillingness of the worshiper to admit that he is a "miserable sinner," "there is no health in us," "the burden of our sins is intolerable." Senseless routine, empty ceremonial, subjective effects, and humanistic preaching will always cause a short-circuit. The sincere worshiper in a dedicated congregation will discover that "God moves in a mysterious way" and sometimes his ways are also very slow.

Worship is action. It is action on God's part as he works through the channels of our response to him. It is action on our part as we turn to him in faith, making the decision to trust him, throwing ourselves on his mercy, and intending to be obedient servants. The classic prayers state some of these intentions: "Whose service is perfect freedom. . . . Defend our liberties and fashion into one united people the multitudes brought hither out of many kindreds and tongues. Take away all hatred and prejudice, and whatever else may hinder us from godly union and concord. . . . Grant us grace fearlessly to contend against evil, and to make no peace with oppression. . . . Incline the heart of employers and of those whom they employ to mutual forbearance, fairness, and good will."

The story is told of the person who went to a Friends' Meeting for the first time. The silence continued for about fifteen minutes, and finally he whispered to his neighbor, "When does the service begin?" and the answer was, "When you go out that door." Worship is action: it is the service of God in terms of glorifying him in praise and thanksgiving, but it continues out of the door into the world as obedience to his will.

WORSHIP AND EDUCATION

If "education is the experience of the learner under guidance,"[2] the experience of being in a congregation at worship is educational, for here we have a vivid experience directed by the historical customs of the Church and interpreted by the leaders. Children and adults know themselves as members of a worshiping fellowship; they grow up and continue to grow because they are nurtured within the framework of worship.

Here is an opportunity for some of the most significant education that a congregation can develop. Here, at the center of the Church's life, we can be educated to be the Church. The only way to learn to worship is through worshiping, and not just by talking about it. Everything must be done to provide meaningful participation.

When children worship according to their age-levels, much can be done to make it meaningful through their participation in both the leadership and the responses. But there is a difference between "playing church" and "worship through play." With very young children, especially, their games can be a form of worship, or if not always a form at least a means leading to worship. They have a sense of the unseen, think in terms of fantasy, and use their imaginations. This makes them capable of an attitude of reverence, although care must be taken that awe does not disintegrate into dread.

As children grow older, they can be introduced to more adult forms of worship, including a more intricate vocabulary. Whereas in communication, words need a fairly exact meaning in relation to experience, in worship words with a mysterious content can be used to evoke feelings of awe and wonder. The use of liturgical formulas, therefore, are significant because they condition children for the response they need to make in an act of worship. The problem here is to distinguish between words which are meaningless and words which point toward mystery. Too often the words are misunderstood by the children,

2 "The curriculum of Christian religious education is the experience of the learner under guidance." *International Curriculum Guide, Book I* (Chicago: International Council of Religious Education, 1932, 1935), p. 18.

who may say, "Our Father who aren't in heaven, Hallowe'en be thy name," feeling strongly their participation in the congregational act of worship but mouthing syllables only vaguely connected with the mystery to which they point. I am not sure that they gain much from singing about "Gladly, the cross-eyed bear." But the main experience is that of participating in a congregation which is worshiping, for they share the atmosphere before they grasp the words. This leads to the conclusion that adults must be present and must sense the reality of their own worship as they participate with the children.

When departmental worship is used, it is hoped that the children will grow up into the liturgical practices of the local congregation and will find them meaningful. The older youngsters, therefore, will have freedom to experiment with their worship, both in their departments and in their youth groups, and yet there will be a norm in sight for them, a norm which they already know through their participation in the services for adults. Often, however, the worship of the young people is far more vital and relevant than that of the adults, and there is disappointment when they come to the age when they no longer are members of the youth division. This leads to the primary point: the worship of the Church is educational, and it is the vital element in the spiritual growth of the members of the parish.

It is hard to lay down rules for worship, because we share many traditions and because we have many needs. The basic elements in worship are the same for all, and therefore it is essential that the fulness of Christian worship be included: praise, confession, absolution, listening to the Lord through hearing the Bible, affirmation of faith, petition, intercession, offering of self and possessions, preaching of the Word, and blessing; but these elements must always have a dual purpose, pointing to the God in whom we live and move and have our being and to the world in which we live. There must be mystery and relevance, awe and obedience, direction and communion. There can be no such thing as an *audience* listening to prayers, anthems, and sermon; there can only be a *congregation*, the *ekklesia,* responding to the "calling out" of God in prayers and hymns and offering.

We must solve this problem on the adult level as well as on the children's level. There is a sense in which the quality of life

permeates the worship, which is shown by the communal response of the congregation to the reality of God; but there is a
deeper and profounder sense in which the worship of the congregation determines the quality of life of its members. The priority
of God is self-evident in worship, and therefore we get the commandments in the right order: "Thou shalt love the Lord thy
God . . . and thy neighbor as thyself."

There are many rich traditions in our liturgical history, some
of which have been lost by default, some of which have become
overladen with routine, and some of which simply do not speak
to man's condition in the twentieth century. Our antiquarian
liturgical scholars are right in returning to these traditions, but
we need contemporary theologians to determine which of them
might effectively be reborn in this twentieth century. There is
an aptness in the Elizabethan prose of Thomas Cranmer which
makes it suitable for worship in many traditions where English
is the common tongue, but attempts to imitate Cranmer's magnificent style may lead to solemnity and absurdity. To combine
our traditions with modern developments takes a kind of
liturgical ability which is difficult to find in the modern scene.
However, the fact that suitable modern prayers can be written
is evidenced by those of William Bright, Edward Lambe Parsons,
John W. Suter, Boynton Merrill, and others. Some of the twentieth-century hymns and tunes are far superior to those of the
previous century, as can be shown by the hymns of Harry Em-
erson Fosdick, John Oxenham, Jan Struther, and Percy Dearmer
and the tunes of Ralph Vaughn Williams, Martin Shaw, and
Harry Burleigh. New discoveries and experiments in the non-
liturgical Churches illustrate that modern worship can be vital
and relevant. But more needs to be done.

FAMILY WORSHIP IN THE CHURCH

"Those whom God has joined together, let not man put
asunder." In the name of grading worship and classes for
children, the Church is often guilty of sundering family relationships. The unity of the Christian family on Sunday is often
limited to the trips to and from church.

The family-as-a-unit has its basis in Christian faith. There is
an organic unity of the family based on biology, on social forces,
and on God's intentions. This unity exists to some extent in the
home, but outside forces have with increasing pressure made

inroads on this sense of belonging together. Schools have recognized this, at least to the extent of providing organizations for parents, of having visitors' days, and of going to the homes of the children who are having major difficulties. There is increasing emphasis on the significance of the home as a basis for social and personal morality. Studies in character education lead to the conclusion that the key to the problem is parental cooperation. The feeling of cohesion within the family community is essential to a sound Christian education, and one of the most important opportunities for developing this cohesion is when the family worships together in the church.

During the period of concern with the needs of age groups, a proper emphasis was placed on closely graded lessons, which are still the most effective kind for class work. Normally these lessons were divorced from any kind of parental cooperation and from worship. Many denominations have become concerned about this as they have recognized the significance of the parents in the total development of the child. Quarterly magazines for parents, family books, parents' classes, and family nights have become common. But no means were developed for having parents and their children worship together in a service suitable for them all.

A genuine family worship service is especially tailored to the family-as-a-unit. Beginning at 9 or 9:15 A.M., it lasts about thirty-five minutes. It has all the proper ingredients: call to worship, confession, promise of forgiveness, Lord's Prayer, responsive reading, Bible readings, prayer, offertory, sermonette, benediction, with hymns at the proper places and possibly an anthem. The order and customs are those of the major service of the congregation. The service is *modified but not mutilated.* It is not a form of "opening exercises" but is genuine worship in the church.

The values of such a service are many: the family sits together, and the children and their parents witness to their faith within the worshiping community; the children see their parents admitting their sins to a loving God; the family shares together the power of the Holy Spirit as he dwells among them in worship; corporate loyalty to the Church as "our" Church is strengthened; the family feels that each member is important in the life of the parish; because the proclamation of the Gospel is made relevant to each member of the family, no one feels left out (as so often happens with children in an "adult" service). Furthermore, this experience of common worship is carried back into the home, as a basis for discussion and decision; the presuppositions of the Gospel become relevant as possible presuppositions of Christian living in the home, as children and parents fortify each other in their discipleship; opportunity is made for the family to explore the meaning of their life together.

To achieve these values, certain precautions must be taken seriously. This is not "watered-down" worship; it is full-fledged worship for the family-as-a-unit. However, parents are supremely interested in their own children, and what is good for the children is therefore good for the parents. This sets the tone for the worship. We can make use of informality, simplicity, humor, and dignity.

On March 2, 1869, Horace Bushnell preached a sermon entitled, "God's Thoughts Fit Bread for Children," and near the end he said, "I think I see it now clearly: we do not preach well to adults, because we do not preach, or learn how to preach, to children. Jesus did not forget to be a child; but if he had been a child with us, we should probably have missed the sight of him. God's world contains grown-up people and children together: our world contains grown-up people only."

Some people think that there must be a "grown-up" sermon after the children have departed. It is my conviction that we must learn how to preach, vividly, concretely, and briefly, to our families. This is not easy, for many adults have forgotten not only how they *thought,* but also how they *felt* as children. The Lord is our Master at this point also, for in Jesus' teaching through story, parable and distilled wisdom we have the proper combination of event and meaning by which God's revelation can be shared, with the meaning already implicit in the recounting of the human relationships. The sense of confrontation and awe and wonder comes as we see God at work in such relationships as we ourselves experience. It is in such preaching as this that the command, "Go and do thou likewise," falls on willing ears.

If you think that parents do not respond to such preaching, try an experiment of preaching to children, and then after a hymn preaching to the remaining adults. Count the number of references to each sermon among the adult comments at the end of the service, and you will find that almost all of them refer to the so-called "children's" sermon. Children and their parents can share in the Christian experience of hearing the Word of God in Scripture and sermon when we are aware of what we are doing. But a good sermon will move from the children's to the parents' levels in its development.

In family worship in the church, we are striving for a feeling of at-homeness. This can be achieved by a proper combination of simplicity of communication, familiarity of routine, and the right proportion of novelty and unexpectedness. The simplicity is achieved by remembering the child's vocabulary; he does not speak or hear King James English and therefore the reading from Scripture should be in a modern translation, preferably the Revised Standard Version, the Smith-Goodspeed American Translation, or J. B. Phillips' New Testament. He also does not know what to look for when he is listening to the Bible, and he can be helped by a brief and relevant introduction to the passage about to be read. Careful selections of stories, or of teachings that are not too difficult, will lead to a sense of anticipation when the practice becomes customary.

Routine is established by having a service with fixed portions and a standard order, with opportunity to participate verbally at many points. But simplicity and routine can become boring, which is why imagination, humor, and novelty are important. When something new is to be added, it should be a featured attraction, with proper increase of expectation and with a helpful interpretation.

It is obvious that such a service places an added responsibility on the minister. Often this is his largest congregation, and it demands a kind of preparation which takes him into new realms of imagination and interpretation. He has not been trained to lead this kind of worship, and sometimes he resents, consciously or unconsciously, this added burden. He may not learn to do it well until he understands the theology and psychology behind this kind of worship. But he may come to the point where it is his favorite service, for here he discovers an unsophisticated and overt response not only to his leadership but to the God whom we worship and adore.

We call this a family service, and therefore it includes everyone in the family. Carriages in the aisles and babies in arms are normal. Their witness is more important than their participation, for they are making clear the Master's saying, "Let the children come to me." And if they make a joyful noise to the Lord with their cries, this particular congregation will understand, and so will their Lord. They may not stay long, and it is customary for those below the first grade to leave during some liturgical break after five or ten minutes, going to their classes or to a baby-care program. At the end of the service, the others go to their classes. The topics in the classes are often tied in with the theme of the family service, and the teachers are notified what to expect.

Quality begets quantity. Congregations which have instituted family services have had difficulty finding adequate space for new classes, or even for space in church. Parents who have *sent* their children are now *brought by* their children. New teachers are drafted more easily because the standards are higher and potential teachers are trained in parents' classes. More families are reached *as families*. Each member of the family learns to believe, "I was glad when they said unto me, We will go into the house of the Lord" (Psalm 122:1).[3]

BAPTISM

The beginning of a child's education in worship is his baptism (or dedication).[4] Baptism is his incorporation into the

[3] See "The Family Worships Together," *Baptist Leader*, Sept. 1957, pp. 5-6, 16.

[4] I am aware of the difficulties concerning infant baptism when we turn to the Church in the New Testament. This, and the current misuse of baptism, has led such theologians as Karl Barth and Emil Brunner to a denunciation of infant baptism. The corporate nature of the Church, however, is based on the covenant of grace; so we believe that God acts through the Church to make the child his own. The emphasis is on incorporation and grace, not on the faith of the individual and the washing, important as these are in the mature decision of the Christian. The purpose of the New Testament, it seems to me, is more fully carried out when infants are baptized and opportunity for decision is given at the age of discretion through confirmation or some other ritual indicating the acceptance of responsibility. See Karl Barth, *The Teaching of the Church Regarding Baptism* (London: SCM Press, 1948); Emil Brunner, *The Divine-Human Encounter* (Philadelphia: Westminster Press, 1944), p. 132; Geddes MacGregor, *Corpus Christi* (New York: St. Martin's Press, 1959), pp. 128-143; Oscar Cullmann, *Baptism in the New Testament* (London: SCM Press, 1950); Donald M. Baillie, *The Theology of the Sacraments* (New York: Charles Scribner's Sons, 1957), pp. 72-90; Horace Bushnell, *Christian Nurture* (New Haven: Yale University Press, new ed., 1948), pp. 102-164. See above, pp. 24-25.

body of Christ by the power of the Holy Spirit. It is an act of God through the Church on the child. He becomes "a member of Christ, a child of God, and an inheritor of the kingdom of heaven." Baptism is a means whereby God declares his relationship to the person, and the congregation which believes this responds with their act of faith. This faith is provided by the sponsors or parents who speak for the child and by the congregation which receives him. "Does this mean that the benefits of the sacrament come to the child in response to the faith of the parents and the Church?" "Yes," answers Donald Baillie, "that is just what it means. And that is just as it should be, and is in keeping with the whole outlook of the New Testament, which has none of our false individualism."[5]

The child is baptized into a fellowship, he is brought into a new environment or atmosphere, and this is a continuing relationship. There is a difference in environment between a community which baptizes and therefore seals the child's membership and the environment which denies this sacrament to infants. Even the secularist, with only child psychology to guide him, can see that infant baptism makes the crucial difference in the loving environment of the child. For in this congregation into which this child has been received, the members have the responsibility to be channels of God's grace. This is sacramental doctrine and good psychology, far removed from magic or sentimentalism.[6]

Donald Baillie also suggests that because faith does not have to precede baptism, one is enabled to *look back* on his baptism as a means of strengthening the faith he develops as he matures. The sign is given, and the *"efficacy* continues working through faith as we look back."[7] The sponsors, parents, and congregation undertake specific responsibilities for the continuing nurture of the infant as he grows toward that time when he can ratify his baptismal vows as he is confirmed or otherwise professes his faith. He has become a member of the body of Christ, not a member of a denomination or of a particular congregation, and his new relationship, says Reuel Howe, "conveys the power of God in Christ for salvation—a relationship of the redeemed and the redeeming; of the forgiven and the forgiving; of those who

[5] Donald M. Baillie, *The Theology of the Sacraments*, p. 83.
[6] See D. M. Baillie, *ibid.*, pp. 86-87.
[7] *Ibid.*, p. 88.

freely give out of what they have freely received; of those who, having surrendered themselves, have become the instruments of His saving love; of those who, though broken and sinful, by Him are used to heal and save. This is what it means to be His Church, the people of God, the new order of the redeemed personal relationship, the reconciling fellowship."[8]

The sacrament of baptism meets the religious needs of the child or adult. He needs to be loved and accepted, and the act of forgiveness mediated through baptism is a token of God's love for him. Having been "grafted into the body of Christ's church," he is accepted as he is by the members of the congregation, and this relationship becomes vital to his life. He needs a structure of law and order, and the Church promises that he will learn the Law, the teachings, the demands of the Gospel, and all else that he ought to know to his soul's health. He needs freedom to grow, and the promise is that he will make his own profession of faith, confirming his baptismal vows, when he reaches the age of discretion. He needs to develop his awareness of the mysterious holiness of God, and he finds this within the worshiping congregation, leading ultimately to the full community of the Lord's Supper.

If baptism is to have these meanings, it needs to be approached with greater seriousness and educational acumen. Crucial to this is the preparation of parents and godparents for their ministry. Parents may be the sponsors, but if so they are acting in a special vocation which is not their normal Christian responsibility. As with all ministries, the important factor is the function and not the status, and parents have their own unique ministry to their children. However, the Church also needs to observe what is going on, and the sponsors (not parents) accept responsibility for checking on the parents. It has been suggested that a special commissioning of sponsors ought to be included in the baptismal service.[9]

Because of confusion over the responsibilities of the sponsors, in many denominations they are no longer used. But where there has been a heightening of the requirements, with the *expectation* that the sponsors should be Christians and willing to assume a long-term religious obligation, the service of baptism has reassumed its role as a sacrament of the whole Church, in

[8] Reuel L. Howe, *Man's Need and God's Action*, p. 57.
[9] See Derrick Sherwin Bailey, *Sponsors at Baptism and Confirmation* (London: S.P.C.K., 1952), p. 135.

which there is a real lay ministry by sponsors and the congregation. Where parents are unable to find sponsors among their friends and relatives, the local congregation often ministers to them by providing sponsors from among its members.

Many Churches today are making three moves to place baptism in proper perspective. First, there is the practice of pre-parental counseling and education, coming during the months of expectation when the parents-to-be are susceptible to the guidance offered by the Church. This includes thinking about the meaning of baptism and about the people who might fulfill the ministry of sponsor. Second, there is the practice of interviews with the parents and sponsors prior to the baptism.[10] These interviews are often conducted by lay people trained especially for this pastoral and educational task. Third, there are parents' classes which are concerned with their vocation as parents, and this helps them as they seek to fulfill their "priesthood of parenthood" after baptism. In all of this there is recognition of the crucial significance of the first few years of a child's life and of the part played by parents in determining his motivation and attitudes in the future. Horace Bushnell believed that "everything depends upon the organic law of character pertaining between the parent and the child, the Church and the child, thus upon duty and holy living and gracious example. The child is too young to choose the rite for himself, but the parent, having him as it were in his own life, is allowed the confidence that his own faith and character will be reproduced in the child, and grow up in his growth, and that thus the propriety of the rite as a seal of faith will not be violated." The child "is taken to be regenerate, not historically speaking, but presumptively, on the ground of his known connection with the parent character, and the divine or church life, which is the life of that character."[11]

Within the worship of the Church, baptism should have an integral part. It is particularly meaningful when it occurs at a family service, especially when an adult is being baptized at the same time as a child, for then the full teaching concerning baptism becomes possible. Always it should involve the congregation in its responsibility to share with the parents the ministry of parenthood. The educational purpose of baptism centers on those responsible for the nurture of a particular

[10] See the discussion of baptism and the house church, above, pp. 73-74.
[11] Horace Bushnell, *Christian Nurture*, pp. 34-35, 96.

child of God, but the whole setting within the worship of the Church makes it relevant repeatedly to the lives of all the people who in faith turn back to their baptism for strength to go forward in Christ's name.

THE LORD'S SUPPER

From the beginning the Lord's Supper was central in the Church's worship,[12] along with a service of praise modeled after the synagogue service, and both were intimately connected with the preaching of the Word.[13] Today both services continue as part of the Church's worship. There are those who wish to eliminate the service of praise or combine it with the Lord's Supper, so that the latter will be the only service on the Lord's Day. Not only the Disciples of Christ but many others hold this view. Calvin and other Reformers assumed that there would be a weekly celebration of the Eucharist.[14] There are others who would stress the significance of the Holy Communion by limiting its frequency to once a month, although there are not many who would return to the custom of only once a quarter. At the other extreme are those who would have a daily Eucharist, but this would be a minority report from a few Anglicans.

The Lord's Supper is rich in its varied meanings, as illustrated in the words to describe it. The Last Supper became the breaking of bread with the apostles or in the apostolic fellowship; it became the Lord's Supper. After New Testament times it became the Holy Communion, the Eucharist, and the "sacrifice" of the Mass. The members of the congregation offer themselves as a reasonable, holy, and living sacrifice, along with the alms and the bread and wine. They make a pledge of fellowship, accepting the covenant relationship with God and his people. They come in penitence and hope for forgiveness. They come into personal communion with the risen and living Lord, although this can only be defined as the "real presence."[15] It is a thanks-

[12] See above, pp. 24-25.

[13] Some would claim that there was only one service combining everything. See John Knox, *The Early Church and the Coming Great Church*, pp. 27-28; Oscar Cullmann, *Early Christian Worship* (London: SCM Press, 1953), pp. 26-32.

[14] See Geddes MacGregor, *Corpus Christi*, pp. 53 note, 181.

[15] Luther's position is defined as "consubstantiation," Calvin's as "virtualism," Cranmer's as "real presence." It is unfair to classify Zwingli's "memorial" as the "real absence." Faith is always a factor in knowing Christ in

giving for all that God has given and promised to them. It is a table fellowship whereby we assert a deeper unity than now exists. The Lord is host. We sing,

> "Come, risen Lord, and deign to be our guest;
> Nay, let us be thy guests; the feast is thine;
> Thyself at thine own board make manifest
> In this our sacrament of Bread and Wine. . . .
> One body we, one Body who partake,
> One church united in communion blest;
> One Name we bear, one Bread of life we break,
> With all thy saints on earth and saints at rest."[16]

The sacrament includes the fellowship, but it is not initiated by the fellowship. The prior act of God in Christ brings us the sacrament. Each Eucharist takes us back to the Upper Room; we are there. We live through that Supper and the occurrences of the next few days. Our memory is not a faded one, for in our religious imagination we are able to recreate the scene, to relive it.[17] What is harder for us to realize is that we also need to recreate the Christian hope of the coming of the kingdom. With the aid of the Scriptures we can look back, but we do not always know that we can look forward: we "proclaim the Lord's death until he come" (I Corinthians 11:26).

> "Feast after feast thus comes and passes by,
> Yet, passing, points to the glad feast above,
> Giving us foretaste of the festal joy,
> The Lord's eternal feast of bliss and love."[18]

This is the framework: memory and hope; taste and foretaste.

The sacrament is not initiated by the fellowship, but it creates the fellowship. The "heavenly table" is a human fellowship meal with the divine Christ as host. We are "one Body." This is

---

Supper. See Elmer J. F. Arndt, *The Heritage of the Reformation* (New York: R. R. Smith, 1950), pp. 115-116; and Donald M. Baillie, *The Theology of the Sacraments,* pp. 91-107.

[16] George Wallace Briggs, *The Hymnal 1940* (No. 207), stanzas 1 and 3. From *Enlarged Songs of Praise* (No. 266). Words printed by permission of the Oxford University Press, London.

[17] See C. H. Dodd, *The Apostolic Ministry,* pp. 234ff.

[18] Horatius Bonar, *The Hymnal 1940,* No. 206, stanza 3.

stressed in the Liturgy of the Reformed Church in America: "For as out of many grains one meal is ground and one bread baked, and out of many berries being pressed together one wine floweth and mixeth itself together; so shall we all, who by a true faith are ingrafted into Christ, through brotherly love be all together one body, for the sake of Christ, our beloved Saviour, who hath so exceedingly loved us; and shall show this, not only in word, but also in very deed toward one another."[19]

Education in relation to the Lord's Supper is complicated by the requirements for confirmation or profession of faith as a prerequisite for one's first Communion. All that needs to be stressed here is that there be education for confirmation and there be education for receiving the Holy Communion. It is likely that children are ready for the Lord's Supper before they are old enough to undertake the kind of discipline necessary for confirmation.

From the standpoint of worship and education, children can best be prepared to participate in the Lord's Supper by partial participation. In those Churches which bring communicants to the altar rail, at family service the entire family comes forward. Those who are not yet admitted to Holy Communion place their arms behind them, and they receive a prayer of blessing (with laying on of hands) instead of the bread and wine. Just as we don't keep children away from the table because there are some foods they cannot eat, so we do not keep them away from the Lord's presence even if they do not partake of the elements. This service, like the family service of praise, is geared to the family-as-a-unit.

PREACHING

Preaching is integral to services of praise and to the sacraments.[20] The important factor in worship is that the living Christ be present, as we believe he is in the sacraments and in other services of worship, and one of the clearest expressions of Christ's presence and relevance is found in the sermon. The saving truth of the Gospel is mediated through the sacraments and through hearing the Bible read and through the affirmation of faith, but it is also mediated through personality. There is a certain transparency about the preacher, for through him

[19] Quoted by Geddes MacGregor, *Corpus Christi*, p. 196.
[20] See above, pp. 25-26.

we come into the presence of God himself, and the Word is broken open.

Preaching is always part of the worship of the Church, and therefore is to some degree the responsibility of the congregation. Preaching is always directed to a congregation and never to an audience. The congregation responds by listening responsibly, even if critically, because the sermon should help the Church to come to conclusions and decisions about its own life. It is so integral to worship that the congregation should expect a revelation from God to break through the preacher's words, and this does not necessarily depend on the excellence of the sermon.

Preaching *to* the Church is proclamation to those who have already heard the good news. Preaching *from* the Church is the proclamation of the good news to those who have not heard, or at least accepted it. But often preaching is a combination of both factors, for the people in the congregation come from the world with the world's problems and doubts, and in meeting their needs the preacher speaks also to the world.

Whether preaching is to adults, to children, or to families, it is always educational. The relevance of the Gospel to the situation in which the members find themselves is the proper orientation. It is the Gospel which is being proclaimed, but nothing is proclaimed unless there is communication.

The message is always based on hope. It is more than a message of redemption, for it is based on the *results* of a redemption already achieved. The basic assumption of all preaching is that God is a living God; he made man in his own image, and his love is expressed through entering personal relations with man, not only through Jesus Christ but eternally through the power of the Holy Spirit. Man is upheld by God's will and is made strong by God's grace.

This is not all that there is to preaching, but this story lies at the center of it. It is again the problem of *theology in the background: grace and faith in the foreground.* Donald Baillie wrote that "we can preach doctrine *incidentally* all the time," even though we are concrete and relevant in what we say. Following the Church year is helpful, even in non-liturgical churches, for it retells the Biblical story. But he would go further and claim that there should be "definite *courses* of sermons on the great doctrines," based on the Bible and related to the problems of daily life.[21] If there is to be education to be the Church, some of our preaching must follow Donald Baillie's example.

TEACHING THROUGH WORSHIP

Education is built into every experience of a worshiping congregation. The community's information and attitude are improved or not, depending on what happens at baptism, confirmation, joining Church, weddings, funerals, and special occasions, as well as at the main ongoing services. This is the experience of being within the community, guided by the reality of the experience, the content of the words spoken, the music, the relationships, and the atmosphere. Every child, youth, and adult who partakes of this experience is to some degree changed by it.

Even a congregation trained to worship cannot plumb its depths. Certainly there are degrees of profundity and reality in worship. We need not only education *in* worship but also education *for* worship. Throughout the life of the parish, the opportunities will arise to interpret its worshiping life, to help people be ready for what goes on in worship, to build expectation in a realistic manner, and to train them in participation. Certainly this should accompany the family worship services in the preaching and the classes, but it is also essential in the services for adults. There is doctrine behind worship, and by the understanding of this doctrine we can participate more meaningfully in the experience. Among the adults, the cell groups and the special conferences can include worship in their discussions.

Talking about worship, however accurate and meaningful it may be, is no substitute for worship. In the worship of the Church, no one is in the grandstand rooting for the choir or the minister, or watching the others at prayer. In worship, one is glorifying God so that he may enjoy him forever, and he is nurtured in his faith through his worship.

[21] Donald M. Baillie, *The Theology of the Sacraments*, pp. 144-147.

CHAPTER VIII

Fellowship

THE Church is a community of the Holy Spirit, in which Christ is at work healing our broken relationships and sustaining us in our faith and obedience. The Church worships God by preaching the Gospel and administering the sacraments, by expressing the life of the covenant community, and by glorifying God and enjoying him in daily life.

We turn now to the Christian fellowship of the local congregation. Paul wrote, "God can be depended on, and it was he who called you to this fellowship with his Son, Jesus Christ our Lord" (I Corinthians 1:9, G). The Elder of Ephesus made this clear when he wrote, "If we say, 'We have fellowship with him,' and yet live in darkness, we are lying and not living the truth. But if we live in the light, as he is in the light, we have fellowship with one another, and the blood of Jesus his Son cleanses us from every sin" (I John 1:6-7, G). The Church in the New Testament was always a fellowship of persons, centered in Jesus Christ and extending to all men. In this fellowship, the members knew the redemptive and sustaining power of God as a reality in their lives. The grace of God was mediated in the fellowship through the ministry of the members to each other.

THE STRUCTURE OF PERSONS

Men become persons within community. This is obvious, and yet we often forget it. The story of the wolf-girl, who had lived among animals from infancy, illustrates that an individual cannot communicate with other persons outside of human community. Her reactions were similar to those of animals; she walked on all four limbs; she could not talk; she "wolfed" her food. When placed in a home with other human beings she could not respond to their suggestions or imitate their way of doing things.

119

An individual isolated on a desert island would not become a person. The factors of environment play upon the particular organism with its unique hereditary elements, and these are combined with the individual's developing freedom of response, and in this process the personality emerges. The personality is potentially present in the individual, and it evolves within the converging forces of human culture. Within a human society, these potentialities can be so hindered that a deformed personality will develop; his chances of staying alive may be jeopardized. He comes to know other persons through relations with them, and in no other way. These relations include resistance, for in interpersonal relations any person is free to give or withhold consent, and in friendship a relationship of freedom is accepted. But often a relationship will be infected with anxiety or be based on non-personal factors.

These are not simply sociological and psychological observations, although they clearly are that. They are theological factors as well, pointing to the activity of a personal God in our midst. The social process of Christian development and Christian education is provided by the Church. Although a sociology or psychology of education is not sufficient to provide a social theology of Christian nurture, it becomes clear that Christian education takes places within a community of persons who are in relationship with each other and with God who is at work among them.

FELLOWSHIP IN THE BIBLE

This idea of community runs throughout the Bible story. Moses was at first a member of the Egyptian community and rose to prominence, but he always kept his relationship to Israel on a higher level of loyalty. He kept both loyalties strong as long as there was no vital conflict, but there was no question which one had priority. When the proper time came, Moses assumed his position of leadership among the Israelites and led them by the grace of the Lord through many hardships in the direction of the promised land. There was a strong sense of loyalty to God, even though in the midst of suffering those of weaker faith would have turned back and thrown themselves on the mercy of the Egyptians. During the years on the desert, the community came into a covenant relationship with God, and in thanksgiving that "by a prophet, the LORD brought Israel up from Egypt" (Hosea 12:13, RSV; see Exodus 13:9), they agreed to keep his ordinances.

Here we see the Law providing the structure of society. Jewish education centered in the Torah, whereby the growing child became acquainted with the customs, mores, and moral values that held society together and gave him a sense of stability. It permeated his home life and his experiences in the synagogue and temple. The Law was the basis for obedience and for survival. Many times when Israel was on the brink of destruction, the Lord had redeemed her. But the Law also stood for judgment on Israel, who had so often been unfaithful. When the Exile destroyed the nation physically, it was not able to destroy the community of those who had faith in Yahweh.

Almost all instruction took place in the home, and anything resembling a school came at a late date in the Jewish development. Furthermore, because the Jews were a people of the book, instruction was oral and the response was in terms of verbal memorizing. They heard what was said and repeated it. But this always took place within the community of home or synagogue or (later) school. The community lived in faith and hope, and this was communicated through the relationships which permeated their national life. Within this community, individuals became persons, with rights, privileges, and responsibilities.

In the New Testament, the Law continued to have significance in the structure of the community. Jesus came "to fulfill the Law and the prophets." Law, however, was transcended by the relationship of grace, for love is greater than the Law. "Love," said Paul, "is the fulfilling of the law" (Romans 13:10, RSV). The fellowship of believers rose to a higher level: "Our fellowship is with the Father and his Son Jesus Christ" (I John 1:3, RSV). Although God's love is prior to man's love for God or man, in experience they are inseparable. At the Lord's Table, "because there is one loaf, we who are many are one body, for we all partake of the same loaf" (I Corinthians 10:17, RSV).

The sense of community which we find in the New Testament was no mere "togetherness" or comraderie. It was described as follows: "There was but one heart and soul in the multitude who had become believers, and not one of them claimed anything that belonged to him as his own, but they shared everything they had with one another. . . . No one among them was in any want, for any who owned lands or houses would sell them and bring the proceeds of the sale and put them at the disposal of the apostles; then they were shared with everyone in proportion to his need" (Acts 4:32, 34-35, G). The rise of the diaconate was for the purpose of caring for widows and orphans; Dorcas was devoted to deeds of charity; Paul took a collection for the poor in Jerusalem.

THE DEEPENING OF CHRISTIAN FELLOWSHIP

One of the primary functions of the Church is the deepening of Christian fellowship. It can be described as a sense of being at-one with our fellows and with God. It is the overcoming of the loneliness and isolation which hinder us in becoming persons. It is the recognition that our own belonging together is dependent on our prior relationship with God. "We love because he first loved us. If anyone says, 'I love God,' and yet hates his brother, he is a liar; for whoever does not love his brother whom he has seen cannot love God whom he has not seen. This is the command we get from him, that whoever loves God must love his brother also" (I John 4:19-21, G).

Martin Buber's familiar "I-Thou" relationship is one way of understanding this. "A person makes his appearance by entering into relation with other persons," says Buber.[1] God reveals himself through persons, and I discover the meaning of my existence through my relationships with other persons and with God. Herbert H. Farmer writes that "personal relations are the very stuff and texture of our existence as persons. . . . It is hardly too sweeping a statement to say that the most frequent and deep-going cause of disharmony and conflict between men is that in greater or lesser degree, for one reason or another, they treat one another, or are conscious—however dimly—of being treated by one another, not as persons, but as things, not as ends in themselves, but as mere means to something else. This is true from the most intimate domestic relationships up to the vast and complex community problems of social and international life."[2]

The recognition of persons as persons, who have the right

[1] Martin Buber, *I and Thou* (New York: Charles Scribner's Sons, 2nd edit., 1958), p. 62.
[2] Herbert H. Farmer, *Towards Belief in God* (New York: Macmillan & Co., 1943), p. 107.

to autonomy within society, is basic for better personal relations, and is essential to our understanding of the Church as expressed in the life of the local congregation. Justice means that every *child* shall have his due, as John Bennett wrote,[3] that he will be given his full significance as a person. When men are one in Christ, there is no distinction between them in terms of status or rank or race or sex or age.

In such a Christian community, there are two forces at work. The first of these is the power of God's forgiveness which heals broken relationships within the group and with God. In the family, for example, parents often forgive their children, and the power of the community is so strong that the one who is forgiven knows he has been restored *in fact*. More often than parents suspect the child forgives his parent and even though the parent may not be aware that forgiveness has been offered and received, it leads to a restored relationship. In the congregation also there are acts of forgiveness which are deeply felt, and the danger comes when the community itself is not sufficiently gracious to make possible the full realization of the forgiving act.

The second way in which God's grace is received is in the strengthening and sustaining of unbroken relationships. The home again provides an illustration: We all know of happy marriages which have run smoothly for twenty-five or fifty years without a break in the relationship. There have been arguments, creative conflicts, and recognition of the right of the other to his own opinions and actions, but because their love has matured both husband and wife are able to transcend differences as far as their relationship is concerned. There does not have to be anything verbal about this, but they recognize that the closeness of their relationship is firmly established and continually sustained by the grace of God. This is the kind of community which is essential for the local congregation to be a fellowship of the Holy Spirit.

Here is something deeper than sociability. It is the recognition that "it is by grace that you have been saved." It is the treatment of another as a "thou" and not as an "it." "It was nothing you could or did achieve—it was God's gift to you. No one can pride himself that he has earned the love of God. The

[3] See John C. Bennett, *Christian Realism* (New York: Charles Scribner's Sons, 1941), p. 79.

fact is that what we are we owe to the hand of God upon us. We are born afresh in Christ, and born to do those good deeds which God planned for us to do" (Ephesians 2:8-10, P). In our fellowship we become channels of grace to each other and to seek to "walk worthy of the vocation to which we are called" (Ephesians 4:1).

CONFLICTING COMMUNITIES

Man's behavior depends upon loyalty to a community. But we belong to more than one community, each of which has its claim on us. Some of these communities are secular, some are non-Christian or sub-Christian, some are neutral, and some are consistent with the aims of Christian living. Men today stand in such communities. A child belongs to a family, a school, a gang, and a church. A business man seeks to be loyal to his company, his club, his neighborhood, his family, and his church.

A boy may grow up in a home in which each of his parents has a different set of values. This may be complicated by the presence of another relative who disapproves of both parents. He goes to a school which reflects his mother's standpoint and runs with a gang which supports his father's. He also belongs to a Scout group which behaves in a way quite different from his gang and to a church school class which behaves in a rowdy way even while speaking of Christian values. Within none of these groups does he find the grace which heals broken relationships or which sustains his friendships. The result is a conflict of loyalties which could tear him apart psychologically, morally, and religiously.

There are many factors in our contemporary culture which lead to the depersonalizing of life. A father who feels like an automaton at work is not likely to throw off this feeling when he comes home. It is hard to put flesh and blood on statistics. It is difficult to combine status with personal concern. Whether one wears a gray flannel suit or overalls, whether one is an organization man or simply a seeker of status, it is hard to get beyond the twin loyalties to *money* and *power*. Jesus brought this conflict into sharp relief: "No servant can belong to two masters, for he will either hate one and love the other, or he will stand by one and make light of the other. You cannot serve God and money!" (Luke 16:13, G).[4]

The point does not need further analysis here. Every group

[4] See my *Be Not Anxious*, pp. 61-72.

demands loyalty from its members on its own terms. These demands often conflict with one another, even to the extent of confusing men's behavior because they try to do what is expected of them in each group. The resulting attitudes and behavior may result in lack of integration of personality, with man being symbolized by a five-ring circus, each ring doing something different either at the same time or in series. This issues in hyprocrisy, with the person conforming outwardly to each group. He behaves in one way on Sunday in church and in another way at his business and in another with his friends. For such an "other-directed" person, to use Riesman's term, the only solution would be to belong to groups with similar outlooks, so that he would have no genuine conflicts.

In the midst of such contradictions, the Church stands for unity of purpose not by withdrawal from the other segments of society but by having a center of loyalty which transcends them. Basil Yeaxlee speaks of a "master sentiment" which gathers all other sentiments into a purposeful unity.[5] A hierarchy of loyalties and purposes begins to develop in a child of about eleven, and his decisions lead toward whatever integrity he may eventually achieve. This integrity, wrote Horace Bushnell, "does not exclude the grace of Christ, or supercede salvation by grace, but on the human side moves toward grace, and is inwardly conjoined with it, in all the characters it forms."[6] The center of loyalty becomes the will of God understood from within the community of the Holy Spirit.

THE FELLOWSHIP OF THE FAMILY

Both Jews and Christians have always insisted on the significance of the family as a basic element in religious education, not only in terms of instruction but in terms of community life. Parents had the chief responsibility in early Judaism and in the New Testament Church. Most of the rules for parents in the New Testament were very simple, dealing with the necessities of life and orderliness in the family. "The New Testament lays down no kind of curriculum of training for the child," writes William Barclay, "knows nothing about religious education and nothing about schools; for the New Testament is certain

[5] Basil Yeaxlee, *Religion and the Growing Mind* (Greenwich: Seabury Press, 1952), pp. 131-146.

[6] Horace Bushnell, *Christ and Salvation* (New York: Charles Scribner's Sons, 1864), p. 190.

that the only training which really matters is given within the home, and that there are no teachers so effective for good or evil as parents are."[7]

When Barclay speaks of being "effective for good or evil," he is talking on the level of community and loyalty. There is an organic unity of the family which is so binding that it determines the basic direction of a child's growth. "The bond is so intimate," wrote Horace Bushnell, that parents are educating their children "unconsciously and undesignedly—they must do it. Their character, feelings, spirit and principles must propagate themselves, whether they will or not."[8] A child's religion, says Basil Yeaxlee, begins in the relationships between parents and child in terms of "the development of attitudes, attachments and repulsions which are primarily emotional" but also release the "deepest driving forces of personality."[9]

On the negative side, it is from parents that children learn to be anxious, apathetic, disparaging, and lonely. It is within the home that the motivation for learning and achievement is destroyed. During the early years especially the parents have complete control, and these are the crucial years. "Let every Christian father and mother understand, when their child is three years old, that they have done more than half of all they will ever do for his character."[10]

During this age of impressions, most teaching will be non-verbal. More communication takes place by means of a caress, the tone of voice, the establishment of good feeding habits, the parents' faith, the atmosphere or orderliness and contentment, and the fellowship of the others in the family than through any kind of pictures, symbols, or words. At the time when mothers have almost complete control, the influence of the father is equally important, for as the child comes to use words, he will call God "father," and Jesus' word for "father" was "*abba*," which a Jewish child used as we use "daddy."

> "As a father is kind to his children,
> So is the LORD kind to those who revere him" (Psalm 103: 13, G)

[7] William Barclay, *Train Up a Child: Educational Ideals in the Ancient World* (Philadelphia: Westminster Press, 1959), p. 236.

[8] Horace Bushnell, *Christian Nurture*, p. 76.

[9] Basil A. Yeaxlee, *Religion and the Growing Mind*, pp. 57-58.

[10] Horace Bushnell, *Christian Nurture*, p. 212.

Parents establish the *direction* of their children's religious growth in these early years, primarily through what Reuel Howe calls "the language or relationships." Through this medium, they are interpreting God to the child and building up his capacity for *future* faith. In so far as the Christian family is a cell of the larger body of Christ, it is "a house church," and therefore it points toward the discernment and commitment which will come at a later date. The child moves from faith in his parents to faith in his parents' faith to a faith of his own shared in the larger community of the Holy Spirit.

As the child grows older, the Christian faith is communicated by other significant adults in church, school, and community. He has intimations of his own faith, but he does not make it his own. He can share in the community that lives by this faith (both home and church), and thus he is nurtured in it so that faith comes naturally and gradually, but only in adolescence can he make the decision that gives him a faith of his own. This commitment cannot be controlled by education in home or church but comes by the free response of the individual to the grace of God. But unless the planting and watering has been done, it is unlikely that God will provide the increase.[11]

The most important thing about Christian family life is the quality of its fellowship. This is more significant than any religious routines, any teaching about religion, any Bible study, important as these things are. It is good to have grace at table, family prayers, and reading from the Bible, but it is notorious that these can have a negative effect when the relationships are already spoiled by lack of genuine Christian love. Such a family fellowship is intimately related to the larger fellowship of the Holy Spirit, and derives its strength from God through the Church. The early Church was right: Christian education begins in the home; but the later Church was right also: parents cannot do the job alone. Parents need the resources of the Church when the job of Christian nurture is primarily theirs, and the whole family needs the Church when the children are old enough to sense the meaning of words and symbols. But because the Church is also a fellowship including baptized babies, there is no time when infants are excluded from the larger fellowship.

[11] See Basil A. Yeaxlee, *Religion and the Growing Mind*, p. 145.

FELLOWSHIP AND EDUCATIONAL RELATIONSHIPS

We are now ready to see the Church as an educational fellowship. Within this fellowship, integration of the personality may reach its highest level, because the source is a personal relationship with God which transcends all natural groupings. This gives a kind of loyalty which can stand up in the face of all competing loyalties without destroying the other groupings into which men are naturally drawn. The Christian home, especially, is intimately connected with the Church in their mutual task of achieving fellowship and in the nurturing of children in the Christian faith. The quality of Church life, as expressed through its activity as a fellowship, determines the degree of integration reached by its members. Within the fellowship of the Church, therefore, we find educational influences of the greatest significance, which need to be understood on their own level of expression as well as in relation to the other functions of the Church which make an educational impact.

The center of the Church's community life is the Holy Spirit, and the mutual relationships of the members come from participation in the gifts of the Holy Spirit. The picture in the New Testament of the Church as a fellowship is the norm for the Church today, even though it must be adapted to the cultural conditions of a new century. We need to be as aware of the presence of the Holy Spirit in our midst as were the earliest disciples. "Where the empirical Church does not exhibit this spirit of fellowship," wrote Emil Brunner, "it merely shows to how slight an extent it is a real Church."[12]

The work of the Spirit in the Church helps us to lead men and women, boys and girls, to recognize the presence of the living Christ. Otherwise, Jesus will remain only a historical figure, creative and heroic, and dead. This is often what happens in state schools when religious instruction is given in a secular atmosphere. The Church is not a memorial society grieving for its departed founder. It is a fellowship of those who know him as the living Christ.

One learns by being in this fellowship. It begins sacramentally

[12] Emil Brunner, *The Mediator* (Philadelphia: Westminster Press, 1947), p. 615.

with baptism, as we have pointed out.[13] But it also starts with the level of fellowship described by the Master, "Let the children come to me." There are many little things that are important to a child. He must feel at home, wanted, and accepted on his own terms. A boy may want to keep his hat on in nursery class, or wear his six-shooters in kindergarten. A girl may want to nurse or baptize her doll. I have known young children to build up strong emotions against the Church on the basis of such trivial things—trivial to adults. A child may learn more through play than through any other activity, and he may use play to attack his more serious problems and work them out.

The fellowship expressed in a "family night" at the Church may be as important as what occurs on Sunday. The task of the Church is to bring children and adults into the parish fellowship, so that they will be aware of groupings other than their class, their department, or their experience in the Church school. The smaller groupings must come together if there is to be a fellowship in which the redemptive and sustaining love of God is related to the total body of the congregation. The Church's fellowship is for all mankind, for all age groups, and for all conditions of men. It is also for all members of the human families in the congregation. We cannot see the full fellowship if we think of ourselves as little bits of mortar in the bricks of the total building. We need a sense of the whole in order to achieve the vitality of the parts, and family night may help us to see the Church organically rather than in terms of layers.

The family night is not important if it is only a technique. The clue to its success is the spirit of the fellowship. Unless the power of the Spirit approaches what the New Testament means by *koinonia,* all such efforts will be in vain. The idea of a parish supper should always be guided by the ideal of the early New Testament love feast or *agape.* It is a fellowship of persons sharing their goods and their gifts as they participate in the love made possible by God through the Holy Spirit.

Smaller organizations have their separate existence and autonomy within the fellowship, because they need to express their own needs and respond to the Spirit in their own ways. This is why there can be cells within the larger body, set up for the purposes of meeting the particular needs of individuals

[13] See above, pp. 24, 110-114.

and groups. A parish without structure would be an unholy hodge-podge, and only an intelligent schedule of administration can organize the congregation to meet the needs of the members. But each person needs to recognize his responsibility to the total fellowship of the congregation and beyond these boundaries to the wider fellowship of Christians in the world.

Within the local congregation, it is possible to achieve not only this kind of organization but also this degree of fellowship. The difficulty comes at the point where self-interest limits the outlook of the group. There is parochialism not only at the level of the congregation but also within the congregation, and sometimes the most effective groups internally are those which tear down the fabric of parish life. In the long run, such short-sighted goals, restricted to the organization or the parish, destroy the fellowship within the group. But it is hard for the small group to become excited about the parish budget; it is more difficult for the congregation to become excited about the denomination or the National Council of Churches; and it is even more difficult to think of fellowship among members of those denominations which belong to the World Council of Churches. It is hard to visualize the more than 600,000,000 Christians in the world. Why should we talk about ecumenical love when we cannot achieve it in the Ladies' Aid Society?

There is, however, a weakening of the lines of community whenever there are barriers of geography, language, or race. By some inverse logic, the local congregation will always find its internal bond of fellowship strengthened when it looks beyond itself and accepts responsibilities in terms of the total body of Christ in the world. As soon as the needs of others can be visualized and personalized, men respond to such needs. Even on a secular basis, we see this in terms of the widespread response of all people to the appeals for funds to eliminate polio, fight cancer, and aid children in other lands. In this sense, the Church lives by its missionary outlook.

Our loyalty to the Church, furthermore, works through and beyond institutional channels. The fellowship in the congregation, which is closely associated with the sense of community in the Christian homes of its members, is always linked with fellowship in the world. Unless the immediate fellowship of the Church extends to other human groupings, it is not going to achieve anything except a false inward peace. That is why

Christians are always to be found in the world, not distinguishable from non-Christians except in terms of the quality of their lives.

THE LAITY IN TWO WORLDS

Loyalty is expressed in terms of membership in a group. The nature of the fellowship determines the standards of behavior. In our present culture, we belong to various groups with conflicting and often contradictory demands. On the basis of sociology, we see these groups as small portions of the total culture, and the individual must adjust as best he can to organizations within the culture. The child, the adolescent, and the adult must make decisions in the midst of these pressures, and he strives for sufficient maturity and integration to become a person of stability and wholeness within this confusing and sometimes disintegrating influence of his environment.

The Church, as a fellowship, stands within this sociological context. But the Church is different from all other human groups, because it is a "peculiar people" in a covenant relationship with the Lord of history. It is marked off because the basis of its orientation is God rather than man. It is a fellowship of the Holy Spirit as well as a community of persons. It is not an ingathering of individuals who happen to be intrigued by the story of a man who became God; it is not a social group for the promulgation of social values; it is not a means for blessing the ways of American democracy, of the National Association of Manufacturers, or of the socialist party. The Church is a fellowship called by God, it confesses that Jesus Christ is Lord of all, and its loyalty to the community is in terms of its relationship to the Father of Jesus Christ. This is the redemptive and sustaining fellowship which demands a loyalty differing in kind from any socially or legally based loyalty. The Christian has a dual citizenship: in this world and in heaven.

The Christian's ethical behavior arises from his understanding of the nature of the Church. H. Richard Niebuhr describes Evangelical ethics under four headings: First, he says it is *"theocentric"* ethics, issuing "out of a positive relation to God, as that relation is established by, through, and with Jesus Christ."[14]

---

[14] H. Richard Niebuhr, "Evangelical and Protestant Ethics," in *The Heritage of the Reformation*, ed. by Elmer J. R. Arndt (New York: Richard R. Smith, 1950), p. 220.

The master sentiment of the self and of the community points toward God. The authority is not the Bible or the Church, but the Lord of the Bible and the Church. Second, it "issues out of *faith in God*. . . . The conduct of life issues out of the central faith, not as conclusions are drawn from premises but as fruit derives from trees."[15] As we are redeemed from distrust and disloyalty by God's grace, our response is in obedience. We are not saved by our faith, but God saves us when we respond in love. Third, faith in God gives us an ethics of *freedom*. Because "there is no fear in love," we overcome our concern and anxiety about ourselves, and as forgiven sinners we find an integration of the self which transcends physical and social values. We become free from the law by our capacity to transcend it. "Creative morality," says Niebuhr, "is not bound by rule, though it knows all the rules. It does not meet the changing situations of life with the repetition of acts found good in the past, but with deeds that meet the immediate situation, recognized as a situation in the kingdom of God."[16] Fourth, it is *momentary* in character. By this, Niebuhr means that because there is faith in God's providence, decisions are in terms of what God desires *now*. Man is free to do the right thing *now*, because the future is God's.

Ethics is a matter of *vocation* arising from the personal relationship between man and God within the fellowship of the Church. It is the response a man makes to live a life worthy of the summons he has received. His loyalty to the Church as a congregation and as the wider community of the Holy Spirit frees him to be obedient to the immediate demands and claims of God on his own life. Thus his response is unique, in that this is God's will for him now, and there is nothing legalistic or universal about it. William Temple wrote that "the principle of divine vocation . . . relieves the moral philosopher from every claim that he should so articulate the conception of moral good as to provide clear guidance for individual action."[17] This makes every ethical decision a religious act, an adventure in the service of God, a "hazard of confident faith,"[18] and an individual responsibility. Because every man has his own individual vocation,

[15] *Ibid.*, p. 222.
[16] *Ibid.*, p. 227.
[17] William Temple, *Nature, Man and God* (New York: Macmillan Co., 1934), p. 410.
[18] *Ibid.*, p. 411.

which is part of God's overall plan, no ethical system can place all Christians in the same formula. The fellowship may help a man find his vocation, as he works through prayer, analysis, and whatever guidance God may give him to find his responsibility as a child of God.

In general, we may say that a man's vocation is to follow his own aptitudes, for God wants him to use these resources in a way that will give joy and satisfaction. But his natural impulses are often primitive and they need to be modified through the educational influences of the Christian fellowship. In this way, one's aptitudes gain a social efficiency which answers the needs of man. The basic motivation, therefore, is not one's natural abilities, but the use of them in the service of one's fellow man. Whatever one does, it should contribute to the betterment of mankind, in terms of all the groups to which loyalty is owed and ultimately to the entire culture. The idea of vocation either must operate in the religious dimension or else it will contribute to the perpetuation of the divisions and weaknesses of our present culture.

The Church as a fellowship provides the social process by which one becomes aware of his vocation, for the Church has the resources whereby God's call may be heard and examined. Every man is called to love God and his neighbor, and this general requirement needs to be expressed in many different ways. Whenever God's will is translated into human terms, it ceases to be absolute and becomes permeated with the relativities of human experience. The Church as the community of the Holy Spirit finds resources to do unexpected things and the individual is guided into his own specific pattern of behavior. Thus, we can see that ethics in the Christian dimension is always a vocational rather than a legal problem. It is centered in God but relevant to the world in which we live.

The early Church was an example of this kind of vocation. Christians lived in the world, but their witness to their faith caused amazement on the part of the pagans. There are no pagan comments on the quality of the singing or the preaching or the educational procedures. The only thing that the pagans could say was, "Behold, how these Christians love one another!"

The *laos* live in two worlds. They are the people of God, but they are also the people of the United States or of China or of Australia. They work for General Motors and at the country store. They teach in secular schools and in church-related schools. They marry and have children. They remain single. They are in the Church, but they make their way in the world. Their vocation is to serve God, and this occurs in their day-to-day living.

They are prepared for this life partly through the fellowship of their families and partly through the fellowship of the local congregation. The experience of fellowship is in itself educational, for this is something that happens to them in community. Fellowship in itself nurtures understanding, devotion, and loyalty, and through the "language of relationships" we can communicate what is meaningful in the Gospel in terms of our daily lives.

God is a reality in this fellowship, a living person in communion with his creatures. Paul Tillich tells us that Christian faith begins with the realization that "you are accepted, accepted by that which is greater than you, and the name of which you do not know. Do not ask the name now: perhaps you will find it later. Do not try to do anything now: perhaps later you will do much. Do not seek for anything; do not perform anything; do not intend anything. Simply accept the fact that you are accepted. This is the experience of grace. Everything is transformed. We are able to hear him as by grace we accept others, who have not accepted themselves or us. Our broken relationships are restored. We may not be better than we were before, but our relationships are transfigured."[19]

It is this experience which makes the community Christian in the New Testament sense. It comes through worship and service, but it comes also through fellowship. Within the educational program of the local congregation, fellowship is an essential and effective function of the Church.

[19] Paul Tillich, *The Shaking of the Foundations* (New York: Charles Scribner's Sons, 1948), p. 162.

CHAPTER IX

The Church's Mission

THE followers of Jesus had become missionaries prior to Pentecost. The seventy were sent two by two to preach the coming of the kingdom of God and it is reported that their mission was a success (Luke 10:1-20). After Pentecost, the preaching continued to include the demand for repentance and the announcement of the coming of a new era, but to this was added the claim that Jesus, who was risen from the dead, was the Messiah. When the listeners had no knowledge of Jesus, the story of his life was told first. Because the disciples insisted on proclaiming this good news to all who would listen, they began to get into trouble, leading to the first martyrdom—that of Stephen. Beginning in Jerusalem, the mission of the early Church extended to Antioch, where the first mixed congregation (Jews and Greeks) was established. Later, the mission to non-Jews came under scrutiny and finally Paul's position became the dominant one.

From the beginning, the Church's mission was to convert others to faith in Christ. This was not its only purpose, of course, and there is danger in asserting that everything the Church does is its mission (just as there is danger in claiming that everything is its worship or its educational task.) If the Church is the Community of the Holy Spirit or the fellowship of Jesus Christ, one of its major functions is to proclaim the Gospel to those who have not heard it and to those who have heard it and forgotten or ignored it.

The amazing fact about this primitive community is the manner and speed in which it spread. Kenneth Latourette has written, "Never in the history of the race has the record ever been quite equalled. Never in so short a time has any other religious faith, or for that matter, any other set of ideas, religious, political, or economic, without the aid of physical force, or of social or cultural prestige, achieved so commanding a position in such an important culture."[1] This was not "foreign missions" but simply the Church's mission to all those who would respond to the message of the Gospel.

Paul's missionary endeavors were successful because of his principle that in every newly established congregation there should be a mutual sense of responsibility. These Churches became self-governing almost from the start. It is likely that Paul had something to do with the selection of the leaders, but from then on he acted in connection with them in the decisions about baptism, worship, and discipline. They sought his help from time to time, as his letters indicate, but once his basic teaching had been done over a period of several months or up to two years, he had to rely on those in the congregation to maintain the faith. The local congregation was responsible from the beginning for its own finances, education, authority, and dicipline. As a missionary, Paul's object was to work himself out of a job and to go on to the next place, without losing contact with those in the congregations he had founded.[2]

MISSIONS TODAY

The missionary task of the Church has not always been at the forefront of Christian thinking, and the greatest expansion of the Church took place in the latter part of the nineteenth century. Much of this activity was conducted by missionary societies which were not always connected as organizations with churches as institutions. At the end of the nineteenth century, the Student Christian Movement was one of the great interdenominational sponsors of missions, operating under the slogan, "the Evangelization of the World in this Generation." By this statement, John R. Mott and his colleagues did not mean that the world would be converted in a single generation but that every man would have a chance to hear the Gospel and that the approach would be a thorough one. There were criticisms from more conservative Christians, and although the great Edinburgh Conference of 1910 was a direct result of this enthusiasm, the war which followed in 1914 put a stop to any ideas of missionary expansion.

[1] Kenneth Scott Latourette, *A History of the Expansion of Christianity* (New York: Harper & Bros., 1937), I, 112.

[2] See Roland Allen, *Missionary Methods: St. Paul's or Ours* (London: Robert Scott, 1912), for the complete story.

Since then, the missionary strategy of Christendom has been re-examined in a number of conferences. In such books as *Re-Thinking Missions,* there was a swing away from the view that Christianity held an exclusive doctrine of God to the opinion that all religions were somewhat alike. But at the same time, there developed a recognition of the place of the Churches in the former missionary areas which were becoming mature, and thus a voice was heard which was relevant to the actual situations in these lands. While Roman Catholics and fundamentalist sects continued to search for converts anywhere in the world, Protestantism was re-examining its theory. At Tambaram, in 1938, under the influence of Hendrik Kraemer, the pendulum swung back to an emphasis on the exclusive revelation of Christian faith. After the second World War, at Whitby in 1947, the churches spoke of "partnership-in-obedience" as they faced the task of reaching the whole world with the Gospel. There was a sense of urgency in 1947, because the delegates knew that the world was in turmoil and that many missionary fields would soon be closed. Nationalism, communism, Roman Catholicism, and resurgent religions were becoming stronger and time was short.[3]

Another change took place at the Whitby Conference. This was a renewed emphasis on the Church as the missionary arm of Christendom. But this led to severe criticisms, for those who knew their history were aware that the Church often seeks its own aggrandizement and salvation rather than the world's. J. C. Hoekendijk spoke of "the Churchification of our thought," and said that the emphasis must be on kingdom-Gospel-apostolate-world.[4] But *where the Church is truly the Church, there is no confusion between Church and kingdom, and therefore the Church sees its mission to the world in terms of an apostolic ministry.*

The International Missionary Council has resources for understanding the whole foreign missionary enterprise. In its proposed union with the World Council of Churches, we will have a central organization through which the denominations can operate with confidence and increased effectiveness. Consisting of national missionary organizations, the International Mission-

[3] See Stephen Neill, *The Unfinished Task* (London: Lutterworth Press; 1957), pp. 146-167.
[4] Quoted by Stephen Neill, *The Unfinished Task,* pp. 20-22.

ary Council during World War II sponsored a program for "orphaned missions" and after the war was able to bring together former enemies.[5]

What seems to be developing is an ecumencial approach to the problems of the Church's mission. Excluding the Roman Catholic Church, the Russian Orthodox Church, and certain Protestant sects, the International Missionary Council and the World Council of Churches represent the major missionary thrust of modern Christendom. But many denominations still operate through missionary societies and some simply have refused to accept their missionary responsibility. Leaders have been known to discourage recruits of first-class ability from seeking missionary appointments. Only as the Churches recognize their responsibility and work to reabsorb their missionary societies, with both the Churches and their societies working on an ecumenical basis, can we hope for a revived and redirected missionary strategy. Furthermore, ultimately the individual Christian must accept responsibility as a witness for Christ before the total missionary outlook of the Churches can be developed, and this includes the need for an increasing number to volunteer for lay missionary service abroad.[6]

The foreign missionary, although he may be termed a "fraternal worker" and be on foreign soil at the invitation of the autonomous local Church, faces confused and contradictory attitudes. The difficulties are different from those faced by his predecessors, but are not insoluble. Some countries are closed to him because of incipient and actual nationalism, which identifies Christianity with the Western colonialism which it is in the process of discarding. In most of these countries there are serious internal problems, partly because of the novelty of self-government and partly because of the difficulties inherent in becoming a democracy on the English or American pattern without time for trial and error and without a basic Christian and probably Protestant background of values. Another set of difficulties arises where totalitarian or communist patterns of government have evolved, for the Church is considered to be an enemy. But there remain in most countries, due to the re-

[5] See Kenneth Scott Latourette, in *A History of the Ecumenical Movement, 1517-1948,* ed. by Stephen Neill and Ruth Rouse (London: S.P.C.K., 1954), pp. 355-373.

[6] See Stephen Neill, *The Unfinished Task,* pp. 200-224.

markable expansion of the past century, Churches which are developing their own means of expressing their faith, and these Churches desire fraternal assistance from the major denominations now in the World Council of Churches. This is the point at which a revised type of missionary planning is relevant.

Just as the Churches of the West have been caught up in their own nationalism and ecclesiastical structure, the Churches which have arisen as a result of the missionary enterprise have caught the same disease. All Churches must be open to the challenge of a new day and face it with a renewed imagination and constructive planning through their union with each other.

THE LOCAL CONGREGATION'S MISSION

We have been looking at the Church's missionary task in terms of its world-wide scope. This involves the local parish, because it is related organically to the foreign mission programs of its own denomination and of the work sponsored by the World Council of Churches. The local congregation is the recruiting agency for missionary work as well as the source of financial support. Many parishes have maintained through the years a strong program of enlistment for "full-time Christian service" as well as a constant endeavor to provide support for missionary activities.

This involves the local congregation in missionary education, aimed at providing knowledge, enlistment, and support. In one way or another, such education is going on much of the time, although it may be focussed on one or another aspect of the work during the year. There are plenty of materials made available by missionary boards, educational agencies, and the Friendship Press. Frequently there are units of mission study within the regular lessons for classes and study groups.

The Church's mission is to the uncommitted, wherever they may be. Foreign missions and home missions merely describe the area in which the Church's mission operates. The "heathen" are no more likely to be found on the Fiji Islands than at 42nd and Broadway. The Church's mission involves the work in the inner city, the work in rural areas, the work among migrants, and work among suburbanites. There is no difference in kind, if we recognize in the first instance that everyone has a right to the opportunity to hear the Gospel.

The program of the local congregation begins in the congregation. First of all, there are the new born, not yet baptized, who through their baptism will become members of the body of Christ. This opens the door to their parents, who may or may not have made a commitment to Jesus Christ, and who are responsible for the nurture of their new born child. This program we have already described,[7] but we need to see this ministry within the scope of the Church's mission. This missionary responsibility continues until the child is old enough to make his own act of faith later in life.

There are those who have at one time been active as members of the Church and who now are among the lapsed. A strategy is necessary to locate and interest these people in the life of the congregation. Sometimes they have been active and have drifted away from the life of the congregation and still live within the neighborhood. When a Church is not a "monster parish," it is possible to provide a ministry to such people through the laity of the congregation.

Others have lapsed due to mobility. In fast growing parts of the country, people come from their old haunts and settle down in a new home without making any contact with the Church. They may or may not continue to maintain their membership or pledge in the previous congregation, but they do nothing to make themselves known in the parish of the new neighborhood. Sometimes they have visited two or three local congregations, but they have not sensed that they were welcome and no one came to see them. These are the lapsed who are hard to find even when they live next door to the Church. The anonymity of present-day living means that the Churches have no opportunity to find such people.

A special group of the lapsed are young people who have drifted away from the Church during adolescence. No one has experimented thoroughly with *the ministry of youth to youth* within the parish, and yet this is a point at which the lay ministry may be richly developed. The purpose is not to set up a separated youth organization within a larger organization, but to incorporate youth within the total body of Christ by giving them a genuine ministry within the body. One of their missionary opportunities should be the seeking of lapsed teenagers.

A specialized form of the ministry to lapsed youth is the min-

[7] See above, pp. 110-114.

istry to college students. Significantly, some denominations have kept college work under their division of missions instead of under their division of Christian education. Some students are simply fed up with religion because of what they have seen and heard during their early youth; some have had enough of religious instruction because it has been poorly done; some have been exposed to Church-going in such an irregular manner that no habits have been established; and almost all of them are going through the intellectual discipline of doubting every kind of authority including that of the Church. The Churches have recognized this responsibility and on the whole have organized their mission to college students and faculty on an efficient basis, including the opportunity for the students to be missionaries to their fellows and for the faculty to understand what their witness should be under the trying conditions of teaching in a secular university. Much thinking has been done concerning the place of religion in state and private colleges and universities, and the Churches are cooperating at this level much more successfully than they are on the level of elementary and high school education.[8]

There is always a point of contact with the lapsed, even if all they want to do is to recount their complaints. It is more difficult to find a point of contact with the indifferent, who simply are not curious or interested in the problems of living religiously. They may or may not have a set of values by which they live, but certainly they see no need for Christianity. They do not react to what is being said, and do not respond to what is done. This indifference may be based on anxiety or apathy, which grow out of experiences of dread, or it may be based on an innate selfishness which provides its own satisfactions on a certain level, or it may be a concern for power and money which leaves no time or energy for spiritual things. Although the indifferent may be considered one class in terms of the missionary outlook of the Church, they consist of individuals who are indifferent in many ways and for many reasons. Large portions of the population in amost every country exhibit degrees of indifference.

The Church's mission to the indifferent involves a variety of persons and a variety of approaches. But when the local congre-

[8] See *Religious Education* (March-April 1959), pp. 83-148; Erich A. Walter, ed., *Religion and the State University* (Ann Arbor: University of Michigan Press, 1958).

gation succeeds in being primarily a fellowship of the redeemed who are concerned with the welfare of all, simple exposure to the quality of life of the congregation may penetrate the indifference. Whatever the problems the indifferent person may have, they are of concern to those in the fellowship and therefore are to be looked at with sympathy and understanding. What is the meaning of life as the indifferent person lives it now? What are the barriers which prevent the development of interest in the Gospel? How can the Church help this person to live meaningfully now?

Such an approach involves personal concern, person-to-person relationships, and small groups willing to work together for the good of all. The indifferent are rarely caught up by the glories of worship in a large congregation; this may recapture the lapse but it won't spark any fires in the indifferent. They are wary of being caught up into anything at all; of their own volition they are unlikely to make themselves known; they have a sense of vulnerability behind their mask of indifference and they refuse to unveil their hidden feelings. More than the open arms of a receiving congregation are needed; the searching and grappling arms of an outgoing and indrawing congregation are essential. This may become effective through the ministry of the laity, and it is an essential part of Christian nurture in the Church.

Furthermore, there are those who are the enemies of the Church. On the world scale, the active opponents of the Church include the adherents of most of the other religions, especially the Moslems who have through the years been successful in converting Christians, and the adherents of various forms of materialism and atheism, especially the communists. But in the life of the local congregation it is hard to know who the real enemies are: frequently they are high-placed members of the congregation who are using the Church for their own ends, especially for material gain made possible because of the prestige they have achieved in the Christian community. There are always a few self-styled atheists who speak against the Christian faith, and in some cases they are found on the staffs of the schools. Chiefly, however, the enemies of the Church are the agents of non-Christian and sub-Christian values. They may not think of themselves as enemies of the Church and in some cases may belong to the Church, but in all that they do they are breaking down the values for which the Church stands. It is not easy at this point to list occupations which may have this effect, and there are some who would have a blacklist of occupations not open to Christians, as, for example, school teaching was once closed to Christians because it involved loyalty to non-Christian gods (and this problem of the loyalty oath still haunts Christian teachers today).

The conscious enemies of the Church are those who have deliberately chosen a way opposed to Christian values. They use all their power to break down the Church's faith, to prevent the Church's expansion, and to interfere with the Church's work in other human relationships. This can be seen most clearly in East Germany,[9] where slowly but surely the influence of the Church has been cut down by the power of the state; the Church cannot teach religion in the schools, the Church cannot have schools of its own, the Church cannot print its own books, the Church's catechists have to be approved by a communist inspector, preachers have to submit the manuscripts of their sermons for approval, preachers' children cannot go to school after the age of fourteen, young people who do not participate in the youth dedication cannot continue in school or obtain good jobs. There are enemies of the Church both inside and outside the Churches when political, social, and ethical decisions are made; this is not always a matter of black and white, for often a Christian must knowingly compromise in order to obtain any improvement in a secular world, and often in political relationships events must move slowly. But the racial tensions in South Africa and in the United States have been caused by those who call themselves Christians, and the enmity of many in the colored races to Christianity is due entirely to the failure of the Churches to deal in terms of personal values with the problems of other races.

Finally, there is the Church's mission to the ignorant. This group includes those who have not heard the Gospel and those whose training is such that they cannot participate in hearing it. It includes those of other lands who have not yet had the opportunity to know Jesus Christ, those whose intellectual level is so low that they cannot understand, those whose training is such that they cannot grasp the fundamental meanings of the faith. At this point, missionaries have always sought to break down the

[9] See Karl Barth, Johannes Hamel, and Robert McAfee Brown, *How to Serve God in a Marxist Land* (New York: Association Press, 1959), pp. 11-44. See above, pp. 56-58.

language barrier, sometimes by learning the native language and then reducing it to writing, sometimes by teaching the natives the language of the missionary, and often by a bungling translation of Scripture before the missionary has become expert enough to interpret Christian insights in a foreign culture. This leads to the problem of communication, which is one of the major functions of the Church.

THE CHRISTIAN'S RESPONSIBILITY

Stephen Neill suggests that those who are members of the body of Christ need three conversions: to Christ, to the Church, and to the world as God's creation. They may not come in that order, but all three are necessary for the fully matured Christian to become aware of his responsibility to God and to his fellows. Any one of these without the others can lead to an unhealthy lack of balance: loyalty to Christ can become introverted pietism, loyalty to the Church can become ecclesiastical "churchianity," and loyalty to God's world can become humanitarian activism.[10] The Christian as a missionary, who himself has these three aspects of loyalty in proper balance, will seek out others in terms of the same balance. This is why the missionary must always come from the Church and seek to bring others into the Church, seeing the Church as a community of persons loyal to Jesus Christ in the world.

How can the local congregation approach this problem of the Church's mission and release the power of the Holy Spirit entrusted to it through its members? E. R. Wickham suggests that the model was devised by John Wesley, and that the original Methodist "class-meetings" had resources which are lacking in most modern parishes. In some cases the class-meetings only defined the inner lives of its members, but often they brought together lay people who had a vision of the claim of Christ on their lives with others who were seeking for this claim and others who were newly brought into the fellowship. The groups were small enough so that there was genuine personal relationship, and yet they were sufficiently mixed so that the give-and-take between the members became dynamic and contagious in terms of increased devotion and activity.

"The class-meetings," writes Wickham, "became the strong

---

[10] See Stephen Neill, *The Unfinished Task*, pp. 50-51.

ground-floor structure of the Methodist societies, accomplishing ends that were never envisaged—not only religious and pastoral but also creating vital centres of responsible community life often set in the midst of misery and debauchery. They produced an active and articulate laity—at least great numbers of them— such as no other denomination has produced, not only within the Connexion but in secular society, as the leadership given by great numbers of Methodists in the early Friendly Societies, Trades Unions, and Co-operative Societies shows."[11] The class leaders were laymen who knew how to take Christian responsibility, and it is estimated that there were about 25,000 of them along with other lay officers. New members could be brought into these classes and be assimilated into the community prior to partaking in the larger life of the congregation.

Such small groups are the missionary structure of the local congregation. They may not start as missionary groups; normally they begin as study groups, aimed at the immediate needs of the members; but they move toward a renewed emphasis on the ministry of the laity. They become the means of keeping track of individual members who can become lost in the larger congregation but who are known personally to the members of the group. Such groups work within the congregation to restore the sense of community, they become a "remnant" within the larger covenant people, and finally they become the educating and evangelizing arm of the parish.[12]

Sometimes it is necessary to go out from the congregation in order to gain perspective on what ought to happen within the congregation. The "parish life week-ends" sponsored by the Protestant Episcopal Church provide new insights within a mixed group from several parishes.[13] Retreats, work camps, experiences in lay institutes and academies, and other institutions set up for lay people reach a great number. These lay people come back to their congregations and to their work with a renewed sense of the significance of Christian faith.

When lay people return from such meetings with other lay

[11] E. R. Wickham, *Church and People in an Industrial City*, pp. 268-269. See above, pp. 76-80.

[12] See Tom Allen, *The Face of My Parish* (London: SCM Press, 1954), pp. 68-70; Howard Grimes, *The Church Redemptive*, pp. 107-122.

[13] See my *A Symphony of the Christian Year*, pp. 120-121. See above, pp. 68-72.

people, they are ready to form some kind of a group within the congregation or they return to their already formed groups with a new vision. Such groups will come to a new understanding of the missionary task of the local congregation, which is to minister to the new born, the lapsed, the indifferent, the enemies, and the ignorant in their immediate neighborhood, throughout the world wherever their denomination is able to work, and wherever work is going on sponsored by any other Christian group, especially those in the fellowship of the World Council of Churches. Sometimes these groups will also be recruiting agencies for Christian missionaries, who may or may not serve in foreign lands and who may or may not be ordained.

EDUCATION FOR MISSIONS

Missionary education in the local congregation grows out of a concern for the work of the parish, for the spread of the Gospel from the parish, and for the needs of all people. It begins with faith in Jesus Christ, who is the focal point of our faith and who is the one marking Christianity with a stamp different from all the other religions in the world. The conviction that God has revealed himself uniquely in Jesus Christ is the motive for Christian missions. It does not matter whether the Buddhist or the Hindu or the Moslem has truth on his side; of course he does. But in the fulness of time, God sent Jesus Christ, and this is what makes the difference. To evangelize is to confront men with Jesus Christ, so that they will put their trust in God through him, and by the power of the Holy Spirit live as Christ's disciples in the fellowship of the Church.[14]

The reason that education for missions has fallen on evil days is that the local congregation is no longer a missionary fellowship. Either it has discarded the old idea of missions as identified with Western imperialism, or it has been caught up in the relativism of modern tolerance with its decision that Confucianism is good enough for the Chinese and tribal religions are good enough for the American Indian, but in any case it has not seen the missionary imperative as an absolute claim. Even though it is necessary radically to revise missionary strategy, especially in terms of what is happening in the rising nationalisms of our time, the commission has not changed: to preach the Gospel to every creature.

[14] See my *The Clue to Christian Education*, p. 8.

This understanding of the Church's mission needs to permeate the life of the parish. Certainly we find this imperative in the Church's worship, and especially in some of the great missionary hymns:

"Remember all the people
Who live in far off lands,
In strange and lonely cities,
Or roam the desert sands,
Or farm the mountain pastures,
Or till the endless plains
Where children wade through rice-fields
And watch the camel trains.

Some work in sultry forests
Where apes swing to and fro,
Some fish in mighty rivers,
Some hunt across the snow.
Remember all God's children
Who yet have never heard
The truth that comes from Jesus,
The glory of his word."[15]

Such views need implementation in study and action. The educational procedures can dramatize needs, but the way needs to be made clear so that those who learn of the great commission can find the way to do something about it. The lay ministry to the new born, the lapsed, and the indifferent are possibilities even for young children. We frequently rejoice when we observe the enlistment of a new child because of the missionary endeavors of his friend. The Church school class, when it is small enough and personal enough, can capture the loyalty of a shy child almost immediately. Throughout the Church school, the intimacy of the class, if permeated with the quality of life of the congregation as a community of the Holy Spirit, has tremendous missionary potentialities. When adult groups are controlled as to size and when they operate on a similar basis, the same possibilities are there. But the effort to be outgoing by the members must always be in the forefront of their minds in terms of the great commission.

The Church's mission may be led by the ordained minister

[15] Percy Dearmer, *The Hymnal 1940* (No. 262). From *Enlarged Songs of Praise* (No. 369). Words printed by permission of the Oxford University Press, London.

and he himself may have an evangelistic ministry, but it is his direction of the program that is important. Only as he is able to give his laity the freedom to fulfill their ministries can the local congregation be missionary in the fullest sense. Like Paul, he must trust the lay leaders in the congregation; like Paul, he does not have to be at the meetings of the smaller groups at which major decisions for the group may be made; like Paul, he has the care of the Church and the direction of its policy, but also like Paul he does not steal his people's ministry from them.

The risen Lord said, "Go therefore and make disciples of all nations, baptizing them in the name of the Father and of the Son and of the Holy Spirit, teaching them to observe all that I have commanded you; and lo, I am with you always, to the close of the age" (Matthew 28:19-20, RSV).

CHAPTER X

Pastoral Care

At the end of the Gospel according to Matthew the apostles are told to go into all the world and teach; at the end of the Gospel according to John they are told to "feed my sheep." The elders are told by Peter to "be shepherds of the flock of God that is among you, not as though it were forced upon you but of your own free will, and not from base love of gain but freely, and not as tyrannizing over those in your charge but proving models for the flock; and when the chief shepherd appears, you will receive the glorious wreath that will never fade" (I Peter 5:2-4, G). The idea of the shepherd runs throughout the literature of both the Old and the New Testament:

> "Like a shepherd tends his flock,
> With his arms he gathers them;
> The lambs he carries in his bosom,
> And gently leads those who give suck" (Isaiah 40:11, G)

The gentleness of the shepherd leading his sheep, seeking those who have "nibbled themselves lost," leaving the ninety-nine to seek the one who is lost, provides a significant symbol for the pastoral ministry of the Church. The shepherd is contrasted with the "hireling" who simply does his job for pay, for the shepherd loves his sheep and knows them by name. This is obviously a romantic view, for the sheep are grown for their wool and their meat, and they are protected from their dumbness because they are to be used or eaten.

It is hard to be the shepherd of a large flock. Many years ago in *The Reformed Pastor* Richard Baxter wrote that the flock must number no more than the shepherd or shepherds can handle. God does not demand the impossible of the pastor, and because his flock is made up of men and not sheep he can except that the ministry will be shared by all.

The minister of today's congregation is a priest, preacher, prophet, parson, and pastor. This ministry involves choices concerning priorities. In Acts we read that the twelve decided that "it is not right that we should give up preaching the word of God to serve tables" or "to keep accounts," so others were chosen for the task (Acts 6:2). The pastor may delegate both authority and responsibility for tasks which can be accomplished by lay people, and, as we need to keep asserting, he must not rob them of their ministry.

The way in which the pastor's care is exercised changes with the changing conditions of his flock, of the society in which they live, and of the opportunities of help from other sources. As pastor, he needs to work through other agencies and through other people, so that the best possible care can be provided.

THE INDIVIDUAL IN MODERN SOCIETY

Christianity places a high value on the individual person. This is made clear in the story of the lost sheep and is reiterated in the stories of the lost son and the lost coin. The shepherd *seeks* those who are lost; he does not wait for them to come home. Here is the recognition of the worth of man. He may not be worth much in terms of what he has done, but the revelation of God in Christ makes it clear that God values him. Every man is of equal value in God's sight. God does not show partiality. Yet every man is distinctive in heredity, in environment, and in potential and actual attainments. He is so unique that the very hairs of his head are numbered. It is this value of every man in God's sight which provides the basis for pastoral care. Christ died for all mankind and not just for the select few.

The Gospel presents this view of man as made in the image of God and yet a sinner, for whom Christ died, but man does not experience this evaluation in the world around him. He may know himself as a sinner, struggling against a hostile environment, but he does not know himself as saved and standing under the hope of eternal life. He lives in a world in which the process of living depersonalizes him. He partakes of a culture which values him in terms of his power to produce things, but forgets that the workman is a human being. Standardized education, mass communication, advertizing, and the assembly line have eliminated individualism from the possibilities of his future. He may rebel against this, but there is no place to go.

Until this century, in the United States, there was always the frontier. He could move away from the shackles of the old culture to the adventure and freedom of a culture in process of formation, and he could have a part in the creation of the new civilization of the frontier. But today the frontier is gone, and even the explorations of Antarctica are highly organized military and scientific expeditions. There are still frontiers for the few in the area of atomic physics and explorations of space, but at this level there is no place for the mass of humanity.

To some extent, the American without a frontier still has a past upon which he can call. There is a strong Puritan ancestry built into the American way of life, and even the American who has lost contact with the Church finds this rugged faith of his forefathers a guide to his ethical conduct. But in many cases this faith has become so vague as to be of no value, and as he faces the pressures of life he becomes anxious.

ANXIETY

The anxiety of the modern man has its roots in the surrounding culture, and often it begins in infancy. Harry Stack Sullivan wrote, "The first of all learning is, I think, beyond doubt in immediate connection with anxiety." The infant learns "to discriminate increasing from decreasing anxiety, and to alter activity in the direction of the latter."[1] We can see symptoms of this anxiety at all age levels among those who cannot take a stand on anything, who seek to escape from responsibility, who pose as indifferent when important matters are at stake, and who have discovered the effectiveness on their own egos of disparagement. Those who practice disparagement have usually learned it from their parents, and Sullivan says that he thinks "this is probably the most vicious of the inadequate, inappropriate, and ineffectual performances of parents with juveniles—this interference with a sound development of appreciation of personal worth, by universal derogatory and disparaging attitudes toward anybody who seems to stand out at all."[2]

This interpersonal anxiety on the human level is intensified

[1] Harry Stack Sullivan, *Theory of Interpersonal Psychiatry*, (New York: W.W. Norton, 1953), p. 152.
[2] *Ibid.*, p. 243.

by lack of religious faith. When man lives primarily in a one-dimensional world, he has no answer to the problem of his non-existence, and therefore he cannot face death without anxiety. He can become nothing, and there is no way to escape this fact. This complicates and makes deeper his already existing anxiety, which is a feeling of dread about life as well as about death. He becomes unable to respond to the hope of the Gospel: "Throw all your anxiety on him, for he cares for you" (I Peter 5:7, G).

As he fights anxiety unsuccessfully, so he struggles against meaninglessness, with failure the certain outcome. What he is doing is not always obvious, for as A.T. Mollegen says, "you can do this by being right wing in politics, by getting a job with a big company where there is security, by living in a suburban home, and by being a member of a country club and going to Saturday night dances. Or, you can live in the sensate moment by smoking marijuana, by belonging to 'anti-virgin girls' clubs'; or, by listening to Elvis Presley."[3] These may or may not be symptoms of anxiety or the sense of meaninglessness, but we see chaos, unreliability, and senseless activity shouting at us from stage, screen, and book as well as from what we see around us. Of such people, we can say what the son said of his father in *Death of a Salesman,* "He never knew who he was."[4]

THE FAMILY

The roots of such difficulty are usually but not always in the family. Marjorie Reeves writes that "the adolescent who faces his expanding world with most confidence is not, as a rule, the child who at an early age had to fend for himself in a hostile or in-different world, but rather the one who grew up secure in an assured place of love, and found guides at hand to interpret new experiences as they came to him."[5] In our modern society, many of our basic pastoral problems lie in the family life of Church members.

As family life develops, the husband and wife bring to the forefront the basic elements in their backgrounds. Obviously

[3] A. T. Mollegen, in *The Christian Faith and Youth Today,* edited by Malcolm Strachan and Alvord Beardsley (Greenwich: Seabury Press, 1958), p. 69.

[4] Arthur Miller, *Death of a Salesman* (New York: Viking Press, 1949). See my *Be Not Anxious* (Greenwich: Seabury Press, 1957), pp. 3-81.

[5] Marjorie Reeves, *Growing Up in a Modern Society,* pp. 16-17.

there are many differences even in well matched couples. They bring to their marriage divergent temperamental reactions, cultural patterns with long histories, expectations of social roles for parents and children, and certain elements of normal and sometimes extreme anxiety. There are possibilities of conflict in the areas of religious beliefs and practices, of finances, of value judgments and moral behavior, and of affectional and sexual responses. These are given factors in any marriage and do not necessarily lead to crises.

But crises do occur, and often they become the concern of the members of the Church and especially of the pastor. These strains and stresses in marriage may be due to deviation from expectations in terms of a false image of the other spouse, of inability to cope with the natural conflicts of two individuals living in proximity and working out a new and unique basis of being together, or of activity which seems disgraceful to the other. Other crises occur as the children are born and grow. Often such a family is in despair and does not know what resources exist within its own relationships or within the Christian community to which it is attached.

There are forces of integration in every marriage. Affection does not die easily. Inertia may help for a time. There are strong biological attachments other than sexual. There are some common interests on which the marriage was founded. Beyond these purely human factors is the integrating force of the Holy Spirit, who may not be recognized as present. To some degree God is working through the interpersonal relationships in every family, and therefore faith in God becomes a recourse for the healing of strained and broken relationships. The wise pastor is able to work at this point with the family as a unit as well as with the individuals involved, bringing the Church's ministry to the parents and children together.

But marriages break up and the Church has a responsibility to those who have been divorced. It is a strange fact that the Church, which has succeeded in avoiding legalism on many issues, has insistently enforced the letter of its interpretation of the law in the matter of divorce and remarriage. This is the only area in which some denominations practice excommunication and exclusion. Divorcees, facing all the difficulties of trying to rebuild human relationships after the destruction of the most intimate relationship, find the doors of many Churches closed to them. It seems to me that at this point there is a challenge to the pastoral rather than the legal insights of the church's ministry.

One other group needs to be mentioned. The Church has always been concerned with the aged, but with the trend toward longer lives and toward earlier retirement, the problems of the aged have intensified. The changes in housing arrangements have made it more difficult for young families to care for their old people, and many older people do not think they are ready for special homes. Nursing homes for the aged shut-ins are often gloomy places, even when run by Churches. Here is a whole new area for pastoral work on a much broader scale than before.

TRAINING OF PASTORS

Ordained ministers are given training for the pastoral aspect of their office. They are helped in theological schools to understand the social and political forces affecting individuals and groups, the psychology of personal development including religious growth, and problems pertaining to personality. They do not become amateur psychiatrists, but they do learn something of the skills of personal counseling. They begin to see the pastoral side of their ministry in perspective, in terms of the art of ministering to the sick and of making pastoral visitations in homes and institutions. They know what resources can be found in the secular institutions: child welfare agencies, adoption agencies, planned parenthood clinics, marriage counselors, social welfare agencies, Alcoholics Anonymous, juvenile officers, and many others. Some of them work closely with psychiatrists and physicians.

Life in a seminary may approach the community of the Holy Spirit, so that the seminary is a branch of the Church's life. In the rhythm of worship, study, discussion, and service, the student experiences person-to-person relationships with his fellows and with God. He is under discipline, especially in terms of acquiring knowledge of the Bible, theology, Church history, and many other subjects usually classified under the catch-all title of "pastoral theology." In this latter classification he learns to run a parish, to conduct worship, to preach, to understand his responsibilities in Christian education, to place the missionary task of the local congregation in a total perspective, and to become a pastor. At the same time, he is doing what is called "field work," which means that he is working as a "seminarian" (a person who is half lay person and half clergyman but not ordained) in a parish or in other church work, to acquire the necessary skills for his future work. In some seminaries he undergoes clinical training, which involves him in carefully supervised work in hospitals, mental hospitals, welfare agencies, and parishes.

The seminary, we have said, is a community, but it includes all sorts and conditions of students, no matter how carefully they are screened. Both faculty and students are human beings, with all the limitations and sins of being creatures of the almighty and holy God. Relationships do break down, occasionally dismissal from seminary is necessary, and there are those who rebel against certain aspects of their training. On the whole, however, a high degree of competence is achieved.

There are those in the pastorate who feel the need for additional training. There is now an Institute for Advanced Pastoral Studies, which is for the purpose of providing specialized training on an interdenominational basis. There are many special conferences dealing with mental health, spiritual healing, counseling, marriage, juvenile delinquency, geriatrics, and other special interests.

There are many problems which members of a congregation face, and what is needed is expert pastoral help. This the modern pastor is trained to provide, or to find it in those agencies to which he can turn. He is the shepherd of his flock, responsible to them and for them in the light of his calling and his training. However, all ministers have not had this training, for some of them come into the ministry without having graduated from an accredited seminary, and there are differences in the training provided in the seminaries. But it is the overall picture which is important.

In this area of expert care, the lay person's ministry is limited, unless he has had special training. This is the point at which special vocations need to be recognized. The Christian physician, psychiatrist, counselor, nurse, social case worker, lawyer, and other professionals are competent to offer pastoral services in the light of their expertness that the minister cannot offer. Such people have a specialized lay ministry the possibilities of which have only been partially explored by the Church. Essentially, however, what is needed is genuine interest in other persons, and this comes from grace and not from training and it is part of the vocation of every lay person.

LAY PEOPLE AT WORK

"He has given us some men as apostles, some as prophets, some as missionaries, some as pastors and teachers, in order to fit his people for the work of service, for building the body of Christ, until we all attain unity in faith, and in the knowledge of the Son of God, and reach mature manhood, and that full measure of development found in Christ" (Ephesians 4:11-13, G).

Every lay person has resources for being a pastor to his neighbor. Membership in the body of Christ involves being equipped for the "work of ministry." In this sense, every Christian is his brother's keeper, and he has resources by which he can fulfill this ministry. He is already a member of the body of Christ and receives strength from the Head of the body, especially through prayer and worship. He is ministered to by other members of the body, and therefore he is enabled by the power of the Holy Spirit to become a channel of God's grace to others in the community. By study and education he is directed in this responsibility, so that he is more aware of and sensitive to the needs of others. The healing power of God is released through the members of the fellowship, and this issues in a pastoral ministry each to the other.

Paul Tournier has described the process by which genuine meeting between Christians takes place, something which is other than learning from charts or statistics: "Something of a quite different order takes place, almost without our being aware of it. There is established between us a bond of sympathy and affection, the fruit, in fact, of our sincerity the one towards the other. . . . There suddenly awakes in me the certainty that I am no longer learning, but understanding. It is quite different. It is not the sum of what I have learnt. It is a light which has suddenly burst forth from our personal contact. . . . A characteristic feature is that *he* experienced this inner certainty at the same time as I. He felt that he was understood. More than that: he felt also that he was understanding himself better, and that I was understanding him just as he understood himself."[6]

[6] Paul Tournier, *The Meaning of Persons*, p. 22.

This is personal encounter in love, and it is a possibility for every Christian. It is in this relationship that we can become pastors to each other. Frequently the most important element in pastoral care is for the person in need to have a creative and sympathetic listener: this does not take expertness of analysis or advice but only the basic Christian quality of being concerned enough to listen in such a way that the other feels understood and therefore comes to understand himself better. Many times he does not need advice or direction but only the possibility of clearing his own mind and spirit by sharing with someone else. But for the listener, it may mean a revealing of some of his own hidden secrets as he witnesses to his own faith.

The most dramatic example of this lay pastoral care is found in Alcoholics Anonymous. The "cured" alcoholic is able to minister to others because he knows that he is still an alcoholic although he is redeemed by the power of God. In order to remain in the state of dryness, he is strengthened as he ministers to others, although his motivation is one of thankfulness that he is freed from acquiescing to the compulsion to drink. Only rarely can a non-alcoholic minister to an alcoholic, because the possibility of a genuine personal meeting is discounted in advance by the alcoholic.

The lay person in his pastoral ministry is a sinner calling on another sinner, but both of them are human beings for whom Christ died. Just as the "cured" alcoholic witnesses to his faith by his dryness, so the Christian witnesses to his faith in confessing that Jesus Christ is his Lord and Savior, using whatever language or other means of communication makes possible this witness. It may be only a silent and listening sympathy, or it may be providing direct and practical help, or it may be through exploring doubts, or it may be through an invitation to come to one of the groups within the congregation or to the Church's worship and fellowship.

Much pastoral work is done by lay people without their being conscious of it. The friendly visitation, which may be no more than a social call, is pastoral. Both the minister and lay people often discover that the most effective work they do is this simple act of going to another's home to express their friendship in terms of their common humanity, and (incidentally) of their faith in Jesus Christ. Out of such initial meetings, deeper friendships may develop and opportunities for specific pastoral acts in times of crisis may become possible. Home visitation is often the most effective form of evangelism, for the Church's mission and its pastoral concern are never separated when one is approaching new members. Opportunities for specific instruction may accompany the general educational impact of the call in the home.

An even more informal pastoral concern is often experienced in places where the people work. This area is not often open to the ordained minister, except in cases of special industrial missions which reach a small proportion of the workers. The individual lay person, in shop, store, office, or factory, has innumerable opportunities to be sympathetic, understanding, and helpful. He may be indistinguishable from the non-Christians with whom he works (and this is as it should be) except in his quality of outgoingness and understanding.

Wherever the Christian is, he comes up against problems faced by other people. Both inside and outside the local parish, as he calls in homes or meets fellow Christians in the activities of the congregation, as he travels about the country or at work, if he is open to other people on the level of personal encounter, he is going to enter a pastoral ministry. He may become involved in the healing of broken relationships, in the search for meaning in daily work, in hearing of the simple annoyances of living together, and in the striving of those who are faced with moral problems and deep anxieties or guilt. Sometimes it is a practical and material problem, such as finding sufficient food or financial help. "If some brother or sister has no clothes and has not food enough for a day, and one of you says, 'Goodbye, keep warm and have plenty to eat,' without giving them the necessaries of life, what good does it do? So faith by itself, if it has no good deeds to show, is dead" (James 2:15-17, G).

The individual Christian has responsibility, but he shares this responsibility with the rest of the Church—not only with the local congregation. The Church's larger concerns with social welfare, with refugees, with the poor and the sick, involve us in action as a group, for we need the resources of many Christians in order to fulfill this pastoral ministry. It is important to remember that what we call the social gospel did not originate in ideas of a Utopian society but in the concern for those in society who had not experienced justice. The child labor laws were not enacted in order to protect the labor market but because children were not being given a chance to grow up. The legislation the Church insists on is centered in its concern for the welfare of individuals. It is hard to hear the Gospel when one's stomach is calling so loudly. Because the Church is concerned with persons rather than with things or money or power or prestige, it stands for social justice. And when the Church has become identified with the *status quo,* it has crippled itself as a pastoral force in society.

The individual lay person has other pastoral opportunities. The sick in the parish often need the personal concern of their friends more than the constant attention of the ordained minister, although they need both. When members of the congregation are sensitive to the needs of those who are sick, some kind of control can be worked out so that the sick will be ministered to, without being overwhelmed by the effects of bad planning. The same principle needs to be applied to the pastoral care of the shut-ins and the handicapped and the aged. The Church comes to those who cannot come to the church building through the pastoral ministry of its members. Far too little of this is done in terms of an organized personal lay ministry.

The most difficult and most essential of lay pastoral ministries comes when death occurs. The effectiveness of this ministry depends on all that has gone before, for unless a bond of Christian communication is already established there is nothing to build on when a member faces the death of someone he loves or his own death. The kind of understanding described by Dr. Tournier does not develop in a few minutes, even during a crisis, but depends on a previous relationship of confident understanding. This is why neighbors who have only a social connection with the family are often more knowledgeable in their sympathy and actions than those from the congregation who do not know the people or the situation. But where the local congregation has that quality of life which we have been describing, those members who know the people are best suited to carry out a practical pastoral ministry over a period of weeks or months. The problem of death is not faced and accepted if all that happens is a call from a strange minister and a beautiful burial service.

One other general area of the lay person's pastoral work needs to be mentioned. He is a responsible member of the secular community, and as a Christian he needs to undertake what opportunities there are for genuine leadership in worthwhile backing of pastoral work. Most of the agencies on which the Church depends are supported by money raised in the secular community; Christians should support and take responsibility for such activities as the United Fund, Community Chest, Red Cross, Cancer, Polio, and other money raising programs. In many cases they have opportunities to serve on the boards of the agencies supported by such funds. Often they can work in the YMCA or YWCA, and in other agencies where volunteers are needed. Where their professional training is adequate, their daily work may be in such fields of service. Christians are also concerned with the quality of the schools, care of delinquents, foster home programs, improved housing, and political activity. This is the care of souls, and the Christian citizen has a claim placed on him by his Lord to participate responsibly and intelligently and sacrificially. When Jesus preached in Nazareth, he read from Isaiah:

"The spirit of the Lord is upon me,
For he has consecrated me to preach the good news to the poor,
He has sent me to announce to the prisoners their release and to the
    blind the recovery of their sight,
To set the down-trodden at liberty,
To proclaim the year of the Lord's favor!"
                                (Luke 4:18-19, G; see Isaiah 61:1-2).

To the twelve, he said for them to preach that the kingdom of heaven is at hand: "Heal the sick, raise the dead, cleanse lepers, cast our demons. You received without pay, give without pay" (Matthew 10:8, RSV).

This pastoral concern includes the children. Too often ministers and lay people forget that the children need pastoral care. Jesus said that "whoever receives this child in my name receives me, and whoever receives me receives him who sent me; for he who is least among you all is the one who is great" (Luke 9:48, RSV). Washington Gladden many years ago wrote that when Jesus spoke of his flock, "the lambs were mentioned before the sheep. The true shepherd's first care must be for the lambs. He must not only help to fold them, he must feed them."[7] To take an example, how often are children helped in a pastoral way

[7] Washington Gladden, *The Christian Pastor* (New York: Charles Scribner's Sons, 1898), p. 334; see John 21:15-18.

when a death occurs in the family? They are more likely to be shunted off somewhere, as if there is a conspiracy of silence surrounding this horrid fact of death, and they are not given an opportunity to participate as members of the Christian family and the Christian Church and to share in the faith in the resurrection. But children have all kinds of problems less traumatic than this where they are in need of help, not only from their parents and Church school teachers but also from other members of the congregation.

EDUCATION AND PASTORAL CARE

In the giving and receiving of pastoral care, education is going on. Frequently the most important teaching of all occurs in these life-centered problem situations. If learning takes place as we strive to live with anxiety, certainly more desirable learning takes place when through the ministry of our fellows we learn to "be not anxious." When we are on the receiving end of pastoral care, we are learning all the time. But in the offering of the pastoral ministrations of the Church, we are learning more about the healing power of God and we are reduced to wonder and awe as we see the mighty power of God at work in our own ministries. For we know that behind our own understanding and love of our neighbor is the constant love of the heavenly Father. We may have accepted this intellectually, but through our ministry we discover its reality.

All of this reflects the quality of life in the congregation. If you have succeeded in offering forgiveness as from God, and if the penitent person comes to Church in the hope of being convinced of this forgiveness, it is possible for the congregation to short-circuit the process. William Temple quoted Studdert-Kennedy as saying, "The priest, as the organ and mouthpiece of such a society, could give assurance to the penitent that his sin did not exclude him from this movement of divine forgiveness in the Christian fellowship, but that in virtue of his penitence he was free from it. But where the actual members were selfish, censorious, unsympathetic—there the priest could only declare the divine goodwill to the sinner; he could not in the same way actually convey it, because the selfishness of the society for which he acted blocked its effective flow."[8]

There is Christian education *through* pastoral care, and there

[8] *The Best of Studdert-Kennedy* (New York: Harper & Bros., 1948), pp. 5-6.

is Christian education *for* pastoral care. Christians need to understand the claim on them, the ways in which this demand may be obeyed, and the opportunities which are open to them. This is often dramatized in worship. There may be special Sundays which recognize labor, race relations, family life, mental health, support for funds for social agencies, all of which are tied in with community activities. From time to time, attention may be called to the use of political pressures for better housing, public health, improved treatment of mental illness, or other forms of pastoral care in secular form.

Within the congregation there may be special groups who from time to time are concerned with the activities listed above. Others will be organized for purposes of training the people to exercise their pastoral ministry to newcomers, the unchurched, shut-ins, the handicapped, the children, and the sick. There should be close cooperation with the local council of churches, especially in providing hospital and other institutional chaplains and lay assistants.

In its study, the Church never moves far away from the story of the Good Samaritan, which is concerned with what it means to be a neighbor. We need throughout the curriculum exposure to the great figures of Christian history who have been concerned with the welfare of their fellows. It may be that Florence Nightingale and Francis of Assisi have been overworked, but there are many living today who exemplify the same pastoral concern for others. Albert Schweitzer stands as a giant among the rest because he combines so many aspects of the pastoral ministry with a missionary one, and therefore he becomes a symbol rather than an example. We come to an understanding of our service to the Lord when we remember his words, "as you did it to one of the least of these my brethren, you did it to me" (Matthew 25:40, RSV).

We know that young children catch this pastoral vision of the good neighbor. The trouble is that in the expediency and caution of living in a society of conformists, adults lose this vision. We can keep it alive only through remaining sensitive to the needs of others. But to be sensitive is to suffer, and to be completely sensitive to the sufferings of mankind is to take up the cross, and this we do not want to do. It is easier not to become involved too completely.

"I do not want to serve thee, Lord, but if I must,
Please let it be in some less consuming way.
Why is it that a God must choose to tie
His people to him with the strongest means
He has created? If I am thy child,
Remove from me this burden of thy love
And let me serve thee in a lesser way.
Oh, now I understand why Israel could choose
To be thy servant rather than thy son!
I am too cowardly to be thy child—
Let me, like Israel, serve thee under Law
And find thy love therein. This is too close
For me to stand; thou knowest me too well,
And I can see myself for what I am
Reflected with a damning clarity
Against the measure of thy first-born Son.
Release me, Lord, and let me worship thee
A little farther off, and keep my pride."[9]

This is the point at which we are all challenged. If we live according to law, we can keep our pride, but justification by faith begins with humility. In a church in New York City, as the juvenile gangs come in off the streets, there is a sign, "Let every guest be received as Christ."[10] This can have meaning only when all the members of the congregation seek to be a community in which the redeeming and sustaining love of God is operative in their lives, a community in which young and old alike are accepted as those for whom Christ died.

The individual Christian must remember that he belongs to a visible congregation of faithful people. As one of the sheep for whom the Good Shepherd gave up his life, he has in turn a pastoral responsibility to be a shepherd to others in the flock. It is in this congregation that boys and girls, men and women, are raised up to be God's servants in society. Always we are brought back to the love of God for the individual, and to the Church as the fellowship in which God's redeeming and sustaining love is manifest. We go forth from the Church into the world to be obedient servants of the Great Shepherd.

[9] Quoted by James Cleland, in *The Christian Faith and Youth Today*, ed. by Malcolm Strachan and Alvord Beardsley, pp. 16-17.
[10] See Kilmer Myers, *Light the Dark Streets* (Greenwich: Seabury Press, 1957), pp. 9, 17.

CHAPTER XI

Ecumenicity and the Local Congregation

IF WE believe in the One, Holy Catholic, Apostolic Church, we expect to find it in the local congregation. The most important fact in recent Church history has been the coming together of the Churches in the ecumenical movement, as exemplified since 1948 in the World Council of Churches. William Nicholls has written that "the only way to be Catholic in a divided Church is to be ecumenical." No Church can be fully catholic unless all Churches are united; "Catholicity is thus a dynamic quality, not a static possession."[1]

Ecumenicity exists on many levels of Church experience. Whenever two Christians of differing denominations meet and recognize each other as Christians in terms of their encounter with Christ together, there is ecumenicity. Because they come from different communions or confessions and discover that they are servants of the same Christ, they see that the division of their Churches is a scandal in God's sight. Because we share in the gift of a new relationship through faith in Christ, we belong together even if we are separated. We need to have a visible unity in order to face a divided world. We need an ecumenical community through which to express our belief in the Holy Catholic Church, and we now find that by God's grace we have the beginning of this in the World Council of Churches.

This oneness in Christ exists even if we in the Churches fail to recognize our unity. Christ cannot be divided. We must agree with William Nicholls when he writes, "The saving work of God goes on through the divided churches. Through their ministering of the Word and Sacraments, and through their corporate life, men are still confronted with the living Christ, still initi-

[1] William Nicholls, *Ecumenism and Catholicity* (London: SCM Press, 1952), p. 106.

ated into His eschatological salvation, still built up and sanctified in Him in history. The way into the Body of Christ remains open in the separated churches. The eschatological reality of the Church remains one, and cannot be divided. In our separated Eucharists we receive the whole Christ, and it is the same Christ, whom we all receive."[2] By "eschatological unity," Nicholls means the unity which stands as a promise in the kingdom to come and of which the sacrament of unity is only a foretaste.[3] Our unity exists in Christ as the foundation of the Church and as a promise of the future. But we live in a divided Church, and the claim of God upon us to become one cannot be ignored.

THE EARLY CHURCH

John Knox is right in saying that "the united church of tomorrow cannot be modeled after the divided church of the first century,"[4] but this is only a portion of the truth. The center of the Church's faith is Jesus Christ, and he is one. "Is Christ divided?" asked Paul (I Corinthians 1:13). Even historically the essential unity of God's people has never been completely lost, although it has seemed to the world that the Church consists of packs of competing wolves.

The controversies of the early Church always threatened division. Sometimes there were disputes between members in a local congregation, as when Diotrophes and Demetrius provided contrasting kinds of leadership (III John). Other controversies threatened to split the whole Church in two, as when the dispute over whether to admit non-Jews to baptism without circumcision caused a breach that never was completely healed. False teachers gathered disciples around them. Heresies were combatted by Paul in his letters and by the author of the Fourth Gospel. Out of these controversies, the more or less fluid thinking of New Testament times began to harden, the canon of Scripture began to take form, and the creeds emerged. But with each change, some group was cut off from the rest of the Church. There was a growing unity, but at each stage of early Catholicism a new body of Christians was formed. The later Church had its troubles: at one time in the fourth century there were six bishops in Antioch, each claiming to be the valid suc-

[2] *Ibid.*, p. 97.
[3] *Ibid.*, p. 37.
[4] John Knox, *The Early Church and the Coming Great Church*, p. 16.

cessor to the apostles! "Earlier heresies disappeared or were suppressed; those of the fifth century remain to the present day as a source of unhealed division in the Christian world. The ancient 'Lesser' Churches of the East—Coptic, Ethiopian, Syrian, Armenian, Assyrian—are all to this day either 'monophysite' or Nestorian."[5] The great schism between East and West occurred in the eleventh to the thirteenth centuries, culminating in the destruction of Constantinople during the Fourth Crusade in 1204. Attempts were made to heal this breach as late as 1452. By the time of the Reformation, there were three great and rather unhealthy blocs: Rome, Constantinople and Moscow, and the Lesser Eastern Churches.[6]

On the whole, it is a rather sad story. There were times of great glory, and the Church in the West did succeed in permeating the culture of much of Europe, but whatever power it had was already greatly weakened by both political and religious events prior to the Reformation. Although the Reformation let loose in the world the process of division of the Churches, this was not its purpose or its doctrine. Luther, Calvin, Cranmer and the other reformers were concerned with the unity of the Church and sought for ways to achieve that unity outside of Rome. These leaders were close together in their doctrines, but geography and nationalism were against them. If Calvin, Bullinger, Melanchthon, and Cranmer could have come together, their discussions might have halted the movement toward the development of separate Churches.[7]

Attempts at unity have never died out completely. John Dury in the seventeenth century was an apostle of unity who sought to become all things to all men through ordination in different traditions: Presbyterian, Anglican, and Independents.[8] There were attempts at unity in the next two centuries, but the only successes were across national and not across denominational lines. More success came from the voluntary societies of Christians who worked together without too much concern for denominational barriers and from the mission field.

[5] *A History of the Ecumenical Movement, 1517-1948*, ed. by Ruth Rouse and Stephen Neill, (London: S.P.C.K., 1954), p. 12.
[6] See *Ibid.*, pp. 1-24.
[7] John T. McNeill, in *A History of the Ecumenical Movement, 1517-1948*, pp. 54-58.
[8] See Norman Sykes, in *ibid.*, p. 134.

THE ECUMENICAL REFORMATION

The modern movement toward Church unity began in 1910, with the World Missionary Conference at Edinburgh. There had been earlier gatherings, going back at least until 1854. At Edinburgh two great leaders emerged: Joseph H. Oldham and John R. Mott. Both of them were leaders in the student Christian movements and were concerned with missions and with unity. The conference was missionary and practical in outlook, but it gave rise through the vision of Charles H. Brent to the later conferences on Faith and Order.[9]

As a result of Edinburgh, the International Missionary Council was constituted in 1921. But even more quickly the movement envisioned by Bishop Brent caught fire. The Protestant Episcopal Church in 1910 set up a commission to bring about a conference on Faith and Order. At the same time almost to the day, Peter Ainslie of the Disciples of Christ was instrumental in starting a commission on Christian union. But the direct line to the conference at Lausanne came through Robert Gardiner, a lawyer and a lay man of the Protestant Episcopal Church, who gave of himself voluntarily to establish the Lausanne Conference on a sound foundation. When the conference met in 1927, the most important factor was the profound ignorance of each other's positions. There were many points of agreement, but the Eastern Orthodox, the Society of Friends, and some of the Reformed Churches had serious reservations about some of the resolutions. Certainly the most significant development was the sense of community and mutual confidence.[10]

Between Lausanne and the Edinburgh Conference of 1937 a great deal of study occurred. There was official representation at the 1937 conference from most of the Churches of the world, except from Germany under Hitler. The most difficult subjects were dealt with in terms of both honesty and charity. On the problem of the ministry and the sacraments, always the most thorny topic, D. M. Baillie said that the report was "far ahead of anything the Churches are likely to have reached at present. Is not this the value of these ecumenical gatherings? We have come to discover our nearness to one another, and agreements were reached, not by compromise, but by genuine rapprochment

[9] See Kenneth Scott Latourette, in *ibid.*, pp. 356, 360-361.
[10] See Tissington Tatlow, in *ibid.*, pp. 405-425.

which could not have come about otherwise. If it can happen on the ground of the Ministry and Sacraments, it can happen on any ground; and if it can happen in a Conference such as this, it can happen also in the churches themselves. . . . Something is here happening which is most significant."[11]

The other movement emerging from the meeting together of Christians of all denominations at Edinburgh in 1910 was called Life and Work. The vision of peace among men, seen against the background of the war, led to the Stockholm Conference of 1925. The acknowledged leader was the Archbishop of Uppsala, Nathan Söderblom. There was recognition of the differences between the Churches, but there was also an acceptance of "the responsibility of the churches for the whole life of man."[12] Again, as at Lausanne, there was a continuation committee, and many meetings and movements brought Christians together to consider social and political problems during the intervening years until the next conference at Oxford in 1937.

At Oxford as at Edinburgh in 1937, the German delegation could not be present. There were representatives from the Orthodox and other Eastern Churches, but only a disproportionately small number from the younger Churches in the mission fields. The slogan at Oxford was "Let the Church be the Church!"[13] This motto is open to misinterpretation, but it is a recognition of the place of the Church in the salvation of the world, for if the Church is truly the fellowship of Jesus Christ and we can educate people to be the Church in this sense, there is hope for the world. "The primary duty of the Church to the State is to be the Church, namely to witness for God, to preach His Word, to confess the faith before men, to teach both young and old to observe the divine commandments, and to serve the nation and the State by proclaiming the Will of God as the supreme standard to which all human wills must be subject and all human conduct must conform. These functions of worship,

[11] Quoted in *ibid.*, p. 433, from *The Second World Conference on Faith and Order, Edinburgh, August 3-18, 1937*, ed. by Leonard Hodgson, p. 136.

[12] Nils Ehrenstrom, in *ibid.*, p. 550.

[13] "It is interesting to note that this famous phrase does not appear in the printed Conference material. It occurred in the first draft of the Report on 'The Universal Church and the World of Nations', written by its Chairman, Dr. John A. Mackay, and it reappears in the Message of the Conference in the following form: 'The first duty of the Church, and its greatest service to the world, is that it be in very deed the Church.'" *Ibid.*, p. 591, n.

preaching, teaching, and ministry the Church cannot renounce whether the State consent or not."[14]

We have seen how the missionary movement, the concern for theology, and the work of the Church in the world tended to bring the Churches together in great conferences. There were also great Christian lay movements which have been so important that they should be considered "major allies."[15] The YMCA, YWCA, and World's Student Christian Federation were pioneers in Christian cooperation, and although they are not Churches they have been deeply involved in the ecumenical movement. The World Council of Christian Education and Sunday School Association and the Department of Christian Education of the National Council of Churches in the United States also have advisory relationships to the World Council of Churches.[16] Denominational fellowships and organizations, which more and more cross national boundaries, councils of Churches in various nations, including in some cases actual federations, many journals of an ecumenical nature, and interdenominational theological seminaries must be seen as part of the total picture.

The idea of some kind of league or council of Churches had been in the minds of many leaders throughout these years of increasing Christian fellowship. The two great movements, Faith and Order and Life and Work, could not be kept separate indefinitely, and prior to 1937 a great deal of hard thinking went into the problem of how a council of Churches could be organized. If the Churches were going to "let the Church be the Church," they had to recognize its ecumenical nature. As a result of many meetings throughout the world, the intention became clearer, and after the conferences of 1937 another conference was held at Utrecht in 1938. This basis adopted was: "The World Council of Churches is a fellowship of Churches which accept our Lord Jesus Christ as God and Savior."[17] This was changed in 1960 to read: "The World Council of Churches is a fellowship of Churches which confess the Lord Jesus Christ as God and Saviour according to the Scriptures and therefore seek to fulfill together their common calling to the glory of the one God,

[14] *The Churches Survey Their Task*, p. 82, quoted in *ibid.*, p. 591.
[15] See Ruth Rouse, in *ibid.*, p. 599.
[16] See *ibid.*, p. 612.
[17] W. A. Visser 't Hooft, in *ibid.*, p. 705.

Father, Son and Holy Spirit." William Temple became the chairman of the Provisional Committee. The war of 1939-1945 slowed up the actual formation of the World Council but it led also to a deeper ecumenical fellowship. From the headquarters in Geneva communication lines were kept open between Christians in the warring countries. Before his execution, Dietrich Bonhöffer managed to get to Geneva and Stockholm for meetings; aid to refugees and prisoners of war was handled with a magnificence of which only Churches were capable; plans were made for the post-war settlement. During this period, some of the most important leaders died, including William Temple, William Paton, and V. S. Azariah. Finally, in 1948 in Amsterdam the First Assembly of the World Council of Churches was held, with delegates from 147 churches in 44 countries.[18]

Here was no super-Church, but a council through which the Churches could express their unity in Christ. It is not the only ecumenical movement in Christendom, for many of the other organizations which have assisted in the development of the World Council of Churches have kept their own identity. It does not include all of Christendom, for Rome and the Southern Baptists and many sects refuse to join the fellowship. But within the fellowship can be found frank discussion, information not otherwise available, pastoral and missionary concern on a corporate scale, and witness to unity in Christ. It does not sponsor unions of Churches, but it is the inspiration for them.[19]

When one thinks of the ecumenical movement, he thinks in terms of John R. Mott and J. H. Oldham (both laymen), Archbishops Temple, Söderblom and Germanos, Bishops Azariah, Brent, and Bell, Dr. Visser 't Hooft, Dr. William Paton, and Professor Friedrich Siegmund-Schultze. It has not been a lay movement, even though the leaders of lay movements have been involved. But it has not been a clerical movement either, for the average clergyman has been as isolated as the average lay person. It has been a top-heavy movement of men of vision, who have been the genuine leaders of twentieth-century Christianity, and the roll call of their names is like a list of great saints. But at Evanston in 1954, when a great ecumenical service was held in a football stadium, over 110,000 people were present and Chicago had its worst traffic jam in years.

[18] See *ibid.*, p. 719.
[19] See Stephen Neill, *ibid.*, pp. 728-729.

The recognition of the place of the laity has come with the establishment, in 1946, of the Ecumenical Institute, near Geneva, where there is a graduate school during the winter and innumerable conferences during the summer. It is not exclusively for lay people, but is for all who feel that there is need for "an apostolic type of leadership 'which not only aims at changing the life of individuals, but also seeks to achieve a peaceful penetration into the various sections of the community and the various areas of life.' "[20] The Institute cooperates with other endeavors to set up institutes and conferences for lay people, but chiefly it offers the opportunity for ecumenical encounter to those who attend.

ACTUAL UNIONS

Bishop Azariah once quoted an Indian proverb: "The enmity between first cousins is the hardest to eradicate."[21] But within the larger fellowship, there are families of Churches who might be described as "brothers," and it is in this area that reunion is most likely to occur. Between 1910 and 1952, there were 19 mergers that did not cross confessional lines: Baptists, Presbyterians, Lutherans, Congregationalists, Methodists, and others. There were 15 mergers which crossed confessional lines, such as the United Church of North India (Evangelical and Reformed, Congregational, Presbyterian, and United Church of Canada) , The United Church of Canada (Presbyterian, Methodist, Congregational, Union Churches) , The Reformed Church of France (Reformed, Evangelical Methodist, Evangelical Free) , The United Church of Christ in the Philippines (involving many churches and previous mergers), and the Church of South India (Anglican, Methodist, and South India United Church— including Presbyterian and Congregational). Other Churches achieved full or partial intercommunion. In Switzerland six churches came together to form the Federation of Swiss Protestant Churches. In other areas negotiations were still in progress, some going back thirty or more years. There were conversations between Churches without serious negotiations. At least 18 cases could be listed of negotiations which had

[20] *Ibid.*, p. 716.
[21] Quoted by J. S. Whale, *The Protestant Tradition* (Cambridge: at the University Press, 1955), p. 321.

been abandoned, as between the Protestant Episcopal and Pres-byterian Churches in the U.S.A.[22]

All of these mergers are important, but the most significant is the Church of South India, where for the first time episcopal and non-episcopal ministries were brought together in a single communion without any doubts as to the validity and regularity of both ministries. There was no difficulty from the beginning in the discussions concerning the Bible, the creeds, and the sacra-ments. At the beginning of the actual union, there were five former Anglican bishops who consecrated nine new bishops. All other ministers continued in the United Church without re-ordination. The conscience of each local congregation was rec-ognized so that no form of worship or ministry would be forced on them. All new ministers were to be ordained by bishops and presbyters and all new bishops consecrated by at least three bishops, but for a period of thirty years ministers from any of the previous Churches may be received without reordination.[23] The union was consummated on September 27, 1947, with only two minor groups holding out; a small number of Congregation-alists finally entered the union in 1950, and a few Anglicans are still outside the community. There is a possibility that the Lu-therans and Baptists in the area will join the United Church.

Recognition of the new Church came quickly from the non-episcopal communions involved, but the Anglicans made a confusing response, due primarily to the Anglo-Catholic bloc at the Lambeth Conference. But this plan of union has had an important impact on negotiations of other Churches. The South Indians believe that the greatest sin is the division of Christen-dom and they are willing to risk the ire of some Anglicans in order to achieve their union. They believe that they have estab-lished a model for others to follow.[24]

LAMBETH QUADRILATERAL

In 1870, William Reed Huntington proposed a new basis for union. Much of it was only an invitation for others to become Episcopalians, but the enduring part was what came to be

[22] See Stephen Neill, in *ibid.*, pp. 496-505, for a complete list of these negotiations during this period.

[23] See J. E. Lesslie Newbigin, *The Reunion of the Church* (New York: Harper & Bros., 1948), p. 107.

[24] See Stephen Neill in *A History of the Ecumenical Movement, 1517-1948*, pp. 473-476.

known as the Chicago-Lambeth Quadrilateral. It had four planks as a basis for union: the Holy Scriptures, the two creeds, the two sacraments, and the historic episcopate. Reactions to such a platform were negative, because it seemed to free church-men simply a disguised invitation to give up all that they had fought for. It might be said, however, that in the sixty years between 1888 and 1948, most of these suspicions had been put to rest. The Church of South India has brought all forms of polity together in a system which is consistent with the Chicago-Lambeth Quadrilateral.

Let us look at what is implied: Every denomination has built into its beliefs the acceptance of the authority of Scripture. Anglicans, Lutherans, and Calvinists express their belief in al-most the same manner, and others are not far away in words or meaning. The interpretation of Scripture may vary, but often the greatest variations exist within the limits of a denomination rather than between members of different denominations. There is an authority resident in the first century of the history of the Church which provides a norm for future development. Once this is granted, the added authority of the second century, or the fourth century, or the sixteenth century, or the nineteenth cen-tury is only a matter of difference based on the same essential belief that Holy Scripture contains all that is necessary for salva-tion.

The creeds offer greater difficulty, partly because the degree to which they rest on the Scriptures is not always clear, partly because there is variety of opinion as to whether a creed is a symbol of faith or articles of belief, and partly because there are denominations which have existed for many years without any creedal basis in this sense. Most Churches, whether they use the creeds in worship or not, find the creeds consistent with their own formularies. The creeds represent Christian thinking in the second, third, and fourth centuries as the Church at-tempted to set its own house in order. This does not move the creeds as far away from the Scriptures as we might think, how-ever, for the canon of Scripture was settled during the same period. The minute we move out of the first century, we find the canon of Scripture, the creeds, and the ministry as estab-lished by the primitive Catholic Church. It becomes impossible to reject one without bringing the others (including Scripture) into serious question as an authority.

The sacraments offer no real difficulty until we get involved in the problems of the ministry. Baptism and the Lord's Supper are genuine sacraments of the Gospel and they are mediators of God's grace. The risen Lord is known and his presence is real in the Holy Communion. To define his presence more exactly than this is dangerous, and we must be satisfied with the words attributed to Queen Elizabeth I:

> "He was the Word, who spake it;
> He took the bread and brake it;
> And what his Word doth make it,
> That I believe, and take it."

The historic episcopate is the real cause of difficulty in the Quadrilateral, but H. W. Montefiore says, "the Church of England, in her wisdom, has never made any authoritative definition of the historic episcopate. Such a definition would not only ill accord with the whole Anglican method and ethos. It would not even be possible to make."[25] J. A. T. Robinson makes the same point from another angle: "We affirm that the episcopate is dependent on the Church, and not the Church on the episcopate. We believe its possession to be a necessary mark of the Church's fullness, rather than an indispensable qualification for being a part. It is not what makes the Church the Church—so that in exclusion from it everything falls to the ground. But in repudiation of it the Church can never express the plenitude of its being as the one Body of Christ in history."[26]

John Knox believes that ultimately a place must be found for episcopacy, along with the presbyterial and congregational polities, in the reunited Church. The point is that we already have its functions: spread out in a presbytery acting in its episcopal capacity, in general superintendents, and in a primitive meaning of the term at every celebration of the Lord's Supper. Even in congregational polity, the minister is ordained by his fellow ministers (acting in their episcopal capacity) and not by the laity in

[25] H. W. Montefiore, in *The Historic Episcopate*, ed. by Kenneth M. Carey (London: Dacre Press, 1954), pp. 125-126; see also the magnificent history of ideas of the ministry in the Church of England by Norman Sykes, *Old Priest and New Presbyter* (Cambridge: Cambridge University Press, 1956), and the comments on it in A. E. J. Rawlinson, *The Anglican Communion in Christendom*, (London: S.P.C.K., 1960), pp. 46-52.

[26] J. A. T. Robinson, in *The Historic Episcopate*, p. 22.

the congregation. "The crucial issue, then," concludes Knox, "is not whether we shall have episcopacy simply as such; this we all have, and it is important that we recognize this common possession. The issue is whether we shall accept episcopacy in a special sense: namely, as a distinct order of ministry, superior to the presbyterate and the diaconate, and as standing in a particular historic succession."[27] This obviously does not imply an Anglo-Catholic view of apostolic succession or a view of the Church as defective without the historic episcopate.

The weakness of the Quadrilateral is that it stops at this point. There is a need to recognize the significance of the local congregation, of the place of lay people in the counsels of the Church at every level, and of the doctrine of the priesthood of all believers. The Church of South India has managed to do this. These values existed in the New Testament Church, and Congregationalism has been the most significant form of it in modern times. It belongs to the visible structure of any united Church of the future.

THE LOCAL PARISH AND THE ECUMENICAL VISION

This vision of the ecumenical movement as it operates through the World Council of Churches in Geneva or through the counsels of ecclesiastical statesmen in terms of mergers is hard to keep alive in the local congregation. It is difficult to feel any penitence about a scandal and sin which have existed since the beginning of Church history. The vision of the unity that God intends must be seen against the background of our divisions. A. C. Headlam wrote that "the Church which should be one is divided and of none of the separated bodies can it be said that it represents the full Apostolic tradition. We know that this is the case of every other body but our own; it is obvious that it must be true also of ourselves. . . . It is the bounden duty of all Christians to do all in their power to unite the separated members of Christ's flock, and to build up anew the Body of Christ."[28]

A starting point is the Week of Prayer for Unity. In 1956, the World Council of Churches prepared a Litany which has more than passing significance:

[27] John Knox, *The Early Church and the Coming Great Church*, p. 143.
[28] A. C. Headlam, *The Doctrine of the Church and Christian Reunion* (London: John Murray, 1920), pp. 223-224.

it is both sacramental and missionary, includes proclamation and teaching, is both pastoral and administrative.

This vision of the Church can be held before us because we are the Church as we come together in worship.

THE LOCAL PARISH AND ECUMENICAL RELATIONS

The lines are not always clear, but there is a direct path from the local congregation to the World Council of Churches in Geneva, with two intermediate stops along the way: the local council of Churches and the National Council of Churches; and sometimes there is one other intermediate step, the state council of Churches. But the direct line to Geneva is open, for the publications from there are available in the local church and there are conferences for lay people sponsored directly by the World Council of Churches.

The local congregation can never meet its full obligation to minister to its own environment. The surrounding society is a mixed one, Protestant, Roman Catholic, Jewish, and others, and even the Protestants belong to many different Churches. Therefore, the only way for the Christian voice to be heard, influence to be felt, and service to be rendered is through the local council of Churches. This council can minister to the hospitals, jails, orphanages, and other institutions; it can sponsor the released-time programs in Christian education in the schools and run vacation church schools; it can sponsor programs for migrants, set up ministries in housing areas, and do social service work; it can locate new residents and give their names to the nearest church of their choice; it can run radio and television programs, sponsor special motion pictures, set up community Lenten and Thanksgiving services, do group publicity for the newspapers, and run special conferences for the clergy. The list seems almost endless. All of it is the work of the Churches unified in the council of Churches. This is ecumenicity at the local level, where it is easiest to express it. But even at this level, parochialism is a disease which holds many parishes back from anything more than token cooperation. A good program takes staffing, finances, and close cooperation with all the Churches in the area. This is the point at which the individual lay person can cooperate with those of other faiths in common service of the Lord.

As you enter your church you may see a sign: "This parish

supports the National Council of Churches." The Federal Council of Churches had been formed in 1908 and included most of the major denominations from the start. By 1948 it was involved in a wide maze of activities as it responded to emerging needs. In 1950 it joined with seven other ecumenical agencies to form the National Council of Churches, whose functions include foreign and home missions, Christian education, stewardship, religion in higher education, and women's work. The denominations include the National Council in their budgets, but local congregations add to this with their own gifts.

The World Council of Churches is related to the National Council, but its membership is by denominations and representation on its official committees is by denominational appointment. Its purpose and activities we have already discussed.[30]

ECUMENICAL EDUCATION

The possibilities for education in relation to the ecumenical movement are promising, for much material is now available to guide lay people who want to know about it. But the problem is deeper than this. Because the movement has been primarily on the level of high level talks and conferences, the impact of the movement toward unity has not been felt by either the ministers or the laity in local congregations. Partly this is a matter of information, which is why the story of the ecumenical reformation in this century has been recounted. But chiefly it is a matter of the narrow limits of Christian horizons. With difficulty, Church members can move in their thinking from the local parish to the denomination and even to its foreign activities, but it is much more difficult to become involved in relations with the congregation across the street and its denomination, and almost impossible to imagine what it means when many denominations cooperate on a world-wide scale in matters involving their closer unity. Yet, if we are to become what the Church is meant to be, it is clear that we must turn our educational aims in two directions: First, we must seek to obtain the information that will guide both clergy and laity in their ecumenical thinking, and second, we must seek opportunities for genuine ecumenical meeting on the local level.

First, there are some sources of information which the local congregation can use. For thorough study there is *A History of*

[30] See above, pp. 169-170.

the Ecumenical Movement, 1517-1948, edited by Ruth Rouse and Stephen Neill.[31] There are four volumes of *Documents on Christian Unity,* edited by G. K. A. Bell.[32] For a simpler approach there is *Toward a Reborn Church,* by Walter Marshall Horton.[33] Biographies are available on some of the leaders, including Peter Ainslee, Bishop Azariah, G. K. A. Bell, Bishop Brent, John R. Mott, and William Temple. Current materials may be obtained from the study department of the World Council of Churches. There is a quarterly, *The Ecumenical Review,* which includes news of recent developments as well as articles.

In the field of Christian education, the Division of Christian Education of the National Council of Churches publishes a monthly, *International Journal of Religious Education,* written for lay people, especially teachers and parents.[34] The World Council of Christian Education and Sunday School Association is a federation of autonomous units which through conventions and other projects helps to improve Christian education throughout the world; its journal is a quarterly, *World Christian Education.*[35] The Religious Education Association, founded in 1903, consists of Roman Catholics, Orthodox, Protestants and Jews who are concerned with the improvement of religious education on all levels. Through its local chapters, national conventions, and special commissions it works on religion and public education, religion and higher education, religious education in churches and synagogues, and research over the vast field of religious education at every level; its journal is a bi-monthly, *Religious Education.* The services of its national office are made available to many other organizations, especially as leaders seek widened perspectives, explore frontier problems, and implement ideas.[36]

Second, there are some specific activities. Many projects within

---

[31] London: S.P.C.K., 1954.

[32] Oxford: Oxford University Press, 1924, 1930, 1948, 1958.

[33] New York: Harper & Bros., 1949.

[34] See Gerald E. Knoff, "Christian Education and the National Council of Churches," in *Religious Education,* ed. by Marvin J. Taylor (Nashville: Abingdon Press, 1960), pp. 338-349.

[35] See Nelson Chappel, "The World Council of Christian Education and the World Council of Churches," in *ibid.,* pp. 350-358.

[36] See Herman E. Wornom, "The Religious Education Association," in *ibid.,* pp. 359-370.

the local congregation are related to ecumenical education. For example, a pastor in East Germany has prepared pamphlets with wood-cut portraits of a number of ecumenical leaders. A women's group has prepared a booklet of *Ecumenical Prayers.* Some congregations have experimented at special services with the multi-lingual and multi-faith hymnal, *Cantate Domino,* and prayer book, *Venite Adoremus.*[37] Pictures of ecumenical leaders hang on the walls in the halls of the central office of the World Council of Churches in Geneva, and a gallery of copies could be collected for a local display.

The most important form of education is ecumenical meeting. When a congregation has developed the custom of neighborhood meetings, it is easy to expand their interests to include knowledge of other denominations and to enlarge their membership to include those of other denominations. In such personal discussions, based on actual acquaintance, it is possible to come to a better understanding of the doctrinal and liturgical positions of other churches. Conferences along this same line can be sponsored either by a congregation or by the council of Churches. Let the groups struggle with the issues that divide Christendom, and have reports from smaller committees on the Bible, the ministry, the sacraments, the nature of the Church, the Christian hope. Let them search out their own positions and compare them with others.

The annual week of prayer for unity can be used to turn the thoughts of the whole congregation to the meaning of ecumenicity. Exchange of preachers, mixing of groups for study and prayer, study groups, neighborhood groups, and experiments in ecumenical worship will combine education and the vision of God's purpose for the Church.

In this educational program, we must always be aware that ecumenicity is a matter of life and death for the Churches. This is particularly obvious in the mission field. Bishop Azariah once said, "Do not give us your aid to keep us divided."[38] A divided Church does not witness to a unified Christ, and a Christendom rent asunder cannot be the means of healing the wounds of God's world.

The chief motivation must come from the Church's worship. Not only can there be an ecumenical framework to worship in

[37] Geneva: World Student Christian Movement, 1951.
[38] Quoted by J. S. Whale, *The Protestant Tradition,* p. 322.

the local congregation, but there need to be opportunities for worship in an ecumenical setting. No one attending the daily morning and evening services at the Ecumenical Institute can ever forget the different traditions and languages by means of which the same God is worshiped. Those who have been to ecumenical conferences try to describe what the worship meant, as Douglas Horton did when he spoke of Oxford and Edinburgh, 1937: "In Saint Mary's in Oxford and later in St. Giles' in Edinburgh, where we met daily for intercession, there came to us such a sense of spiritual oneness about the altar of God as to make all who partook of the experience mystically aware of the presence of the Church. That Church, one, holy, catholic, appeared then in its beauty to eyes no longer holden; and all responded to the impulse of the same Spirit. There the richness which is in Christ was poured in lavish abundance and in its many forms of beauty . . . into the souls of the worshippers."[39] But the vision caught in worship is spoiled when we remember that some Christians for reasons of conscience cannot join together at the Lord's Table. The Church that might be will include all Christians at the Lord's Table, and all ministers will be free to act as the celebrant at the Holy Communion. Until then, there will be no sacrament of unity.

[39] "Oxford and Edinburgh, 1937," in *World Christianity*. Fourth Quarter, 1937; quoted in *A History of the Ecumenical Movement, 1517-1948*, p. 589.

CHAPTER XII

Education to Be the Church

THE basic thesis is that genuine Christian education takes place within a Christian community. The quality of life of the community determines the kind of nurture which results. We have indicated that such Christian education is difficult to accomplish in any organization which is not consciously Christian and which does not achieve a reasonably high degree of Christian fellowship. This throws suspicion on religion as taught in secular schools, which, we have said, may well be good instruction *about* Christianity in any of its forms and is therefore valuable as information, but which is not likely to provide the discernment and commitment which emerges in many instances from the grace-faith relationship. Such a process we can hope to find in the Christian home, and this is the point at which all Christian nurture begins. But the Christian family as its best is a cell of the larger body of Christ, and therefore its education points to loyal membership in the Church. The Church, when it truly is the Church, is a community of the Holy Spirit, in which the members experience the redemptive and sustaining power of God through faith in Jesus Christ, and the extent to which the local congregation becomes this kind of a community is crucial to the Christian educational process.

Whatever goes on in the local congregation is educational. It is a question of whether it is education guided by the revelation of God in Christ, with theology in the background and the grace-faith relationship in the foreground, or whether it is something else. It was from this perspective that we looked at the meaning of the ministry and the sacraments, the place of the laity, the Church's teaching, the relation of the Church to the world, the function of the parish, the nature of a class which becomes a group, and the nature of communication. From this same perspective, we looked at the life of the local congregation in terms of its worship, fellowship, mission, pastoral care, and ecumenical relations. In this final chapter, we are to look at the congregation and its program of instruction.

IMPARTING TRUTH

The major task of Christian education is to discover and impart the relevance of Christian truth in such a way that it will be appropriated by the learner and be incorporated into his own life.

Truth is always a representation of reality. A photograph may be an accurate portrayal. But if you are familar with commercial photographers, you know that they touch up a portrait by taking out a wrinkle here, a mole there, a gray hair. The picture looks like the person thinks he looks or would like to look. There are photographers who refuse to do this, but they do not sell many pictures. Often we see more of the spirit of the person in a painting than in a photograph, yet it is not as accurate a reproduction of the physical face.

Truth may be represented in words. It can be found in a written proposition, as in an axiom of geometry. But if we try to understand atomic energy, we have to know about formulas which are not derived from the physics of Newton. There are many kinds of logic, and even the logic of the Greeks can mislead us. We can talk of the "logical impropriety" of religious phrases, as I. T. Ramsey does, because we have discovered that the discernment of religious truth depends on such mixtures of logic. This involves us in a more careful consideration of logic, so that we can better use words for purposes of Christian communication.[1]

Another way of understanding truth is through story, legend, and myth. The value of a story is that through it you can impart information which is relevant to the experience of the listener, and therefore he learns what he as yet could not express in terms of propositions. We have begun to see that some truths of religion are of such a nature that they can only be communicated through the use of myth, for a myth is a story containing a truth which cannot be stated in logical terms. The myth of creation, for example, communicates insights which cannot be contained within a scientific description of the beginning of the world. By studying these myths, we can discover their value as carriers of

[1] See above, pp. 88-91; see I. T. Ramsey, *Religious Language*.

truth and learn their meaning for us today. However, certain myths have become barriers to communication because of our twentieth-century orientation, and sometimes a degree of de-mythologizing may be necessary before we can see the point that is being made.

Sometimes truth seems to remain beyond our ability to apprehend it until we turn to poetry. Poetry, whether it be in the Bible, in our hymns, in our prayers, or in the writings of such Christians as Dante or Browning, Shakespeare or Auden, Wordsworth or Eliot, is the "language of the heart," which Canon Drinkwater calls "poetic-simple."[2]

The difficulties of getting at truth and communicating it are often a matter of vocabulary. The series of cartoons by H. T. Webster entitled "They Don't Speak Our Language" indicated that specialized vocabularies separate us from each other and from the truth we seek. The golfer comes back from his game and tells his wife about how he teed off and how he sliced, and she thinks of hot tea and slices of bread. Yet, as at Pentecost, sometimes the flavor of the words comes through when the vocabulary is strange. "Guys and Dolls" was a hit in London, although the English probably did not understand Damon Runyon's "Brooklynese," but they responded to the color and action and music; they caught the flavor and liked the taste.

We can be introduced to a new vocabulary. This happens every time we attack a new discipline in school. Not only the foreign languages but the sciences challenge us with new words. We take the trouble to learn the vocabulary because it is the only means to the truth we are seeking. When we feel strongly the significance of the Christian faith and belong to the community, we want to know the language of our faith. There are many great words used by members of the community of faith to point toward the saving truth of the Gospel. If we can get beyond and around the unnecessary difficulty of obsolete words and keep the great words, we will be on the right track. What should we do with the following: aforehand, glistering, jot and tittle, neesings, peradventure, wot? These are simply obsolete words from the King James Version of the Bible and have no theological significance. But in time every Christian needs to know: absolution, incarnation, atonement, reconcilia-

---

[2] See above, pp. 91-92; see F. H. Drinkwater in *Shaping the Religious Message*, ed. by Gerard S. Sloyan, pp. 263-280.

tion, redemption, Christology, and many others of a technical sort. They are part of the vocabulary of the Christian family.

The problem with words is two-fold: to guard against using words as ends in themselves, as when the pupil feeds back words to satisfy the teacher without knowing or caring what they mean, and to introduce words in a meaningful way at the proper time. By the time a young person is old enough to be confirmed or to make a confession of faith, he should have a grasp of the basic words of his faith so that they are relevant to his problems of daily living.[3] This leads to the problem of method.

METHOD

Method is simply the means whereby relevant theological truths are connected with the interests, problems, and meanings in the lives of the learners. This is always something dynamic, involving a two-way communication based on the significance of the persons and the revelation of God seen as at work in the process of education.[4]

Conversation is one of the most important methods, because a person can always say, "I don't understand you. Say it again," or "I disagree with you. Let us look at it again." So the teacher comes back in a different way and keeps at it until he is understood. You ask the question, "Who is the Good Samaritan?" and get a blank look from the children, for they have never identified him with this tag-line. But instead of scolding them, you ask another question, "Did you ever hear of a man who was beaten up by robbers?" and they answer, "Yes," and then proceed to tell you the whole story. They knew the answer, but you asked the wrong question.

The same misunderstanding is found among adults. Someone discovers that you are a Christian, and he asks if you think the world was made in 4004 B.C. Or someone will say, "Of course, I'm a Christian, and I believe Jesus was a good man, but I don't go to church." Time and again in our conversations we can clear up such misunderstandings. In the class room, the teacher must use conversation and questions to get at the growing edge of the learners.

[3] See *More Than Words* (Greenwich: Seabury Press, 1955), for an example of a theological word-book for twelve year olds related to their daily experience.
[4] See my *Education for Christian Living*, pp. 159-172.

Another means of teaching is reading. One of the most effective ways of setting up a good discussion is by having reading assignments in advance of the meeting. It is particularly valuable with adults and in leadership training programs. Students will point to ideas in the book which they don't understand, to arguments they disagree with, to subjects which should be developed further, and to concepts which are entirely new to them.

When conversation and reading fail to open up a subject, sometimes a project is in order. By getting involved at this level, perhaps in the area of geography or history, it becomes possible to move into the deeper level of the meaning of it for the participants in the light of what was experienced by earlier Christians.

In all of these approaches, the personal element is paramount. Unless the class has become a group,[5] it is difficult to move into the deeper meanings of Christian belief. A story may be merely a means of entertainment, unless it occurs within the fellowship in which everyone shares the "unsearchable riches of Christ" (Ephesians 3:8). The group feeling may develop as youngsters or adults act out a story or engage in role-play. Discussion always has the potentiality of deepening the sense of personal encounter. A grasp of group procedures by the teacher and observer is often the most important single factor in a successful class session.

Methods are determined by the subject matter and the goals of Christian education. Ultimately, we are concerned about education to be the Church, with all that this means in terms of Christian worship, fellowship, and living. For the children and young people and their parents, the heart of the program of instruction remains the Church school, and this is as it should be.

THE SUNDAY CHURCH SCHOOL

American Christianity cannot rely on the schools to provide religious instruction. This is a handicap which might be overcome along lines consistent with the doctrine of the separation of Church and state, for the task of the schools (if the argument in this book is accepted) is to provide that factual information by which the student appreciates the values of his culture, including those in the Jewish-Christian heritage. But it is not the job of the school to replace the Church, and where the schools

[5] See above, pp. 76-80.

do a good job of religious instruction and the Churches do not meet the nurturing responsibility, loyalty to the Churches is likely to evaporate. It remains the job of the Church, no matter what happens in the schools, to educate its people to be the Church, and this falls primarily on the Church school as an integral part of the life of the local congregation.

The Church school has moved a long way from its beginnings in Gloucester under the inspiration of Robert Raikes at the end of the eighteenth century, and it has moved in this twentieth century in America into a position of almost sole responsibility for the Christian nurture of those of all age levels. The family, if it is to be Christian, must rely more on the Church than it did a century ago in the time of Horace Bushnell. The Church, therefore, is ministering to the family-as-a unit. The basic organization for achieving this is the Sunday Church school.

We have suggested, therefore, that the Sunday Church school be organized primarily in terms of the family-as-a-unit,[6] with special concern lest the individual who comes without his family not feel fully accepted as a member. This implies that there should be worship as part of the program, organized for the family-as-a-whole, with all members participating in the same worship, preferably under the pastor. This is their experience of the Church at worship, in which they learn to glorify God by glorifying him.

Continuous with their worship is their class experience. The opening gambit in class may refer back to their experience in worship (and teachers can be helped at this point by careful advance planning in leadership training meetings). The class, as we have hopefully said, is a group in which there is personal encounter and in which the members are helped to find the meanings of their daily lives in terms of the Gospel.

Such a program does not demand any radical reorganization of congregational life. It requires only that congregational life be made consistent with the demands of the Gospel, and that the care involved in providing this consistency come from sound organizational principles. This is the nucleus of the educational program, and it may be extended to include classes for others in the parish.

[6] See above, pp. 106-110.

Throughout this book we have stressed the significance of the laity. One of the most significant ministries of the laity is that of teaching. Once the quality of life in the congregation reaches a level where God's grace is mediated, the contagious enthusiasm of the teacher in the class room becomes the most significant factor in the educational program. He is more important than the lesson materials or the techniques, for he must seek that capacity to love and accept his pupils as they are, to remember that Christ died for each of them, to provide an atmosphere which has a dependable and reasonable structure of law and order, to recognize the individual capacities of each student and to guide his growth into that freedom which is perfect service, and to point beyond himself to the Redeemer whose grace makes it all possible. The teacher must hold intelligent beliefs, must be capable of leadership, must arouse admiration, and must be committed to Jesus Christ. If a teacher *thinks* he qualifies on these terms, it is proof that he fails to meet the requirements, for then he will be guilty of the sin of pride; but if he is aware that he falls short, then by God's grace he may be called to teach.

In the letter of James, it is said, "Not many of you should become teachers, my brothers, for you know that we who teach will be judged with greater strictness" (James 3:1, G). This states the degree of liability facing every teacher. It is the reason why it is not wise to ask for or accept volunteers. It is my contention that all teachers should be drafted, that they should be selected for their dedication and potential competence, and that the requirement of additional training should be included in the original invitation to teach. This invitation should come after proper consideration by a responsible and knowledgeable committee. "For the Holy Spirit and we have decided not to lay upon you any burden but this indispensable one" (Acts 15:28, G).

We can never escape from the fact that parents have the primary and chief influence on their children. The policy of the Church school must always take into account the potential in properly prepared parents. What happens at Church school can easily be undone by what parents say and do when the children return home as well as by what they do prior to the child's departure; but when parents and children come together to the Church, and during the program parents are helped to understand the nature of their continuing ministry to their children, the vocation of parenthood will begin to take its rightful place again in the larger Christian community. What we need to accomplish is the sense of the family *in* the Church and the Church *in* the family.

INSTRUCTION

If the Sunday Church school is properly the most significant of the Church's educational functions, we must be careful to recognize that it is only one among many. We never get far away from the need for instruction. There is much that is exciting and relevant in religious instruction as such. Where this is offered in the schools, the Churches have less responsibility in this area and are therefore free to place more emphasis on Christian nurture. But the local congregation is never free from the responsibility to encourage knowledge of the faith. The educational program of the local congregation, therefore, operating through all of the channels which we have been describing, and especially through small groups brought into existence for this purpose, should include the opportunity for study and discussion. Perhaps in no area are denominational departments more prolific than in the production of materials for adult education. Much of this is excellent, interesting, and relevant, but too often it is unread. This is not the fault of the material, for it is admirably suited to the needs of the adults for whom it is written.

Adult education has spread like a forest fire throughout the country, and it has invaded the Churches to a certain extent. Some Sunday Church schools have a large proportion of classes for adults. Bible courses have been offered in adult classes in public high schools and have been enthusiastically welcomed. But the problem remains: adults need to be offered not only an opportunity to participate in an educational program in the Church, but also the motivation that comes from a feeling of vitality and a sense of relevance. This can be developed only within a community of the Holy Spirit, in which the content of instruction is seen as significant in the life of the community.

We see this among the minority: those who go to summer camps and conferences, who are already motivated and therefore are ready for a certain amount of hard work, lectures, reading, and discussions. With such adults, we find that the content can be on a level as high as that of college students. They will read serious books written by and for theologians. They will dig into history. They will read their Bibles and the commentaries. They will do enough research to be competent leaders of discussions.

This enthusiasm existed in the class meetings of John Wesley's early Methodists. It is the motivation that leads to the Bible study found today in many cells that meet in neighborhoods and enlist Church members from their own area. It operates to a great degree independently of the clergy, although the ministers know what is happening and work closely with the leaders when necessary.

A PRACTICAL PROGRAM

The reality of the argument in this book lies in the fact that much of what is described here is already happening. What is suggested is a practical program based on a sound view of the nature of the Church as found in the local congregation. There are congregations with an internal discipline that makes possible a deep devotion on the part of their members. There are congregations with weekly meetings of Church school teachers, who work together to come to a fuller understanding of the faith and the means of communicating it to their pupils. There are congregations with a program for parents-and-children-together in which eighty percent of the children bring at least one parent every Sunday. (A few congregations make a demand that enrollment of children depends on enrollment of parents). There are congregations with worship so vital that it permeates the personal relationships of the members and issues in the kind of fellowship described in the New Testament. There are congregations in which the laity and clergy have worked out a proper division of labor, so that there is a fulfillment of the Church's ministry. There are congregations in which parents are fully enlisted prior to the baptism of their children. There are congregations with a great number of cell groups operating in terms of Christian community to discover their responsibility to the world around them. The list can go on, for the evidence is abundant.

But a program, to be practical in the Christian sense, must always see the connection between the tree and the fruit. That is why the Christian must see the theological basis of his good works, must understand the relation between faith and action, must see what the Church is in order to be the Church. All of the activities listed above and many others may lack effectiveness simply because they are not seen in the perspective of an adequate doctrine of the Church. The groups, valid in themselves, may become isolated from each other because we do not understand what a Christian congregation is.

On the other hand, when the Church has been most vital, it has been oblivious to the questions we have been facing. For when the Church is truly the Church, it does not need to stop and ask the question, "Who are we?" The individual Christian, when he knows himself to belong to Christ in the Church, ceases to be anxious about the answer to the question, "Who am I?" He knows who God is, what God intends for his people and therefore for him, and so his task is to be worthy of his vocation.

But in times of stress and strain, when the Church is not sure of its function in the world or when its function seems to have shifted from the major emphasis in the New Testament, it is necessary to take stock, and to look again at the nature of the Church and to discover how to find the Church in the local congregation. "What makes a genuine recovery of Biblical images so difficult," writes Paul Minear, "is the fact that the church's powers of creating and using such images must be restored before the picture language of another century begins to make sense. This fact holds true especially for New Testament images of the church."[7] Then we can put such problems in the background and get down to the main purpose, which is to discover God's will and do it in the world. For the Church does not exist to examine and perpetuate itself, but to be God's people of the covenant, serving him who is Lord of history in the world he has created.

Today, we need to re-examine the nature of the Church so that we can educate people to be the Church. But always education to be the Church has been the chief task of Christian education, for when we get behind the institution and discover that our loyalty is to God through being a member of God's people, we are on the right track.

THE LIMITS OF EDUCATION

Education has definite limits. When it is conceived in terms of instruction, with its main emphasis on facts, it may by accident lead beyond the reception of information, but its pur-

[7] Paul S. Minear, *Images of the Church in the New Testament*, p. 17.

pose is served if the factual information is accepted and understood in a purely horizontal dimension. When it is conceived in terms of activity, participation in the solving of problems is what achieves the goal, with whatever additional understanding may be needed for approaching the next problem. Factual information is acquired and made relevant in the environment; it is still horizontal, but is also social in its implications.

When education is conceived in terms of nurture, of participation in a community in which God is active, it still has limitations. Christian education can tell the story of God's redemptive love in history, can hold out the hope of forgiveness and reconciliation, can present the promise of the abundant life, can point to the hope of eternal life, and can provide the fellowship which by God's grace is both redemptive and sustaining. Such education can change ways of learning, can motivate socially acceptable behavior, can stimulate the learning of facts within the community, can explain the meaning of events, and can present situations in which the relationships between the "I" and "thou" are inescapable. But as Paul wrote, "I planted, Apollos watered, but God gave the growth. So neither he who plants nor he who waters is anything, but only God who gives growth. He who plants and he who waters are equal, and each shall receive his wages according to his labor. For we are fellow workmen for God; you are God's field, God's building" (I Corinthians 3:6-9, RSV).

We always come back to the grace-faith relationship which stands at the center of the Christian life. We see this life as existing within the community of the Holy Spirit, and our power is to bring all men to this community, let the community envelope them, and through the channels of grace vouchsafed to the community they have freedom to respond. "For by grace you have been saved through faith; and this is not your own doing, it is the gift of God—not because of works, lest any man should boast. For we are his workmanship, created in Jesus Christ for good works, which God prepared beforehand, that we should walk in them" (Ephesians 2:8-9, RSV). We can lead pupils into the community, and within the community we can lead them to the edge of the abyss, but only by God's grace do they make the leap of faith. When they make this decision, they know that we are beside them, supporting them by the act of faith which we have already made.

One way of putting this is to say that there are six steps in the Christian commitment: a person must know, feel, worship, decide, join, and act. He can be nurtured through the first three steps, but in the moment of decision he must take a personal risk, knowing he is surrounded by the members of the total body but that he alone is responsible, and then he becomes free to join and to act, and by action he becomes fully a member of the body.[8]

Within the fellowship of the Holy Spirit, the educational process begins with a sense of being a part of an institution, which we identify with the building and the people; this is our first experience of the structure of the community. We become acquainted with its architecture and its organization in so far as it affects us. But unless the sense of personal relationships pervades this structure, the experience is doomed from the start.

The *local church is the place where we become conscious of the beginning of our Christian nurture.* It is here that we see the Bible as a book, the pastor as a leader, the Lord's Table as a table, the class room as having four walls, the paintings and blackboards, and all the rest. We are very much aware of the physical appointments, for it is within a building that certain things are going to happen. The kind of building may to some extent color the nature of the fellowship, but it is essential to realize that the nature of a Christian fellowship does not depend on externals. The first Sunday school of Robert Raikes took place in a house not a church. I have known Sunday school classes to meet in the teachers' automobiles because the storefront church was too crowded. However, children are sensitive to their surroundings and there is no excuse for drab rooms or dull basements or other ways of indicating on a material plane that nothing of importance is happening.

It is the quality of life within the building that counts, and this speaks directly to the youngest children, who are sensitive to the atmosphere around them. Within this fellowship, the pupils learn facts, begin to see the Bible as a drama of God's mighty acts, and seek for an interpretation of this wonderful person, Jesus Christ, who was a friend of little children. Here they learn to worship God.

[8] See A. Victor Murray, *Education into Religion* (New York: Harper & Bros., 1954), p. 14; see also my *Education for Christian Living*, pp. 330-332.

Always we must seek to get behind the form to the reality of God in our lives. We find God through the common ministry of persons to each other within the community. A creed, for example, may be merely a statement of intellectualized concepts, or a body of beliefs to be dissected by the vultures of thought, or a symbol of genuine faith. Studdert-Kennedy wrote that "if our creed is only a form, that may be our fault, not the creed's. You can bet on this—*you don't really believe your creed until you want to say it standing at spiritual attention with the roll of drums in your ears, the light of love dazzling your eyes, and all the music of a splendid world crashing out a prelude to its truth.* If your creed is dull, it is dead, or you are dead, and either one or the other must be made alive again. Either you must change your creed, or your creed must change you. That is the problem that faces us—are we to change the Christian creed, or is the Christian creed to change us?"[9]

Christian character develops within the fellowship. When we are loyal to God, who works within the fellowship and at the same time stands over it, we have a framework for our loyalty that transcends the immediate cultural situation. Our beliefs guide our actions, and our membership in the group is the channel of grace whereby we are able to approximate God's will for us through our vocation. Ethical behavior is our thanksgiving for God's grace to us through Christ, and by the power of the Spirit we are enabled to fight under God's banner and to continue Christ's faithful servant.

TO BE THE CHURCH

We have been called into fellowship with Jesus Christ and with one another, and within this community which is the *ekklesia* and *koinonia* we know ourselves as persons in a personal relationship with God and with each other. In such a relationship Christian education can and does take place. The home, the school, and some community activities assist the Church by providing experiences which may be evaluated in terms of the Gospel. All institutions, including the Church, are always corrupted by sin, but within the Church the purifying power of God is at work to help us appropriate the saving truth of God's work in history and in our lives. Loyalty to Christ

[9] From *Food for the Fed-up*, in *The Best of Studdert-Kennedy* (New York: Harper & Bros., 1948), pp. 32-33. Italics his.

within the community provides the basis for the integration and maturity of the believer, who finds the meaning of his existence through membership in the worshiping congregation. Within this fellowship of the Church, God works to heal our broken relationships and to sustain and strengthen the love of each for the others.

This provides the environment for the communication of the Gospel. Without love we may "speak with the combined eloquence of men and angels," and "stir men like a fanfare of trumpets or the crashing of cymbals," and it would "amount to nothing at all" (I Corinthians 13:1, 2b, P). We are brought back to the personal meeting in the fellowship of love as the only context for understanding God's love, to the fellowship of the family in which the child experiences love before he knows any words, to the fellowship of small groups of Christians among all the larger secular organizations, to the redemptive and sustaining grace of God found in the Church when its members are truly the body of Christ.

Education to be the Church starts with the Church and exists in the Church, but it exists for God and ends with God, and because it ends with God it ends with the promise of the coming of his kingdom in which all men will be brothers.

Books to Read

ON THE CHURCH

DONALD M. BAILLIE, *The Theology of the Sacraments.* New York: Charles Scribner's Sons, 1957.

The view of the sacraments held by many in the classical Protestant tradition.

KARL BARTH, *The Teaching of the Church Regarding Baptism.* London: SCM Press, 1948.

A significant interpretation of baptism, leading to the rejection of the baptism of infants.

EMIL BRUNNER, *The Misunderstanding of the Church.* Philadelphia: Westminster Press, 1953.

Treats the New Testament Church as a fellowship of the Holy Spirit, but is suspicious of any institutional structure.

RODERICK DUNKERLEY and A. C. HEADLAM, eds., *The Ministry and the Sacraments.* London: SCM Press, 1937.

One of the classical statements on the ecumenical problems of the ministry.

BURTON SCOTT EASTON, *Early Christianity.* Greenwich: Seabury Press, 1954.

The early Church in Acts and other essays on the subject.

JOHN KNOX, *The Early Church and the Coming Great Church.* Nashville: Abingdon Press, 1955.

A picture of the early Church and its significance for today, with real concern for the Church in New Testament times.

HENDRIK KRAEMER, *A Theology of the Laity.* Philadelphia: Westminster Press, 1958.

One of the few books dealing with this significant problem.

PAUL S. MINEAR, *Horizons of Christian Community,* St. Louis: Bethany Press, 1959.

Makes use of New Testament imagery to give a startling view of the early Church.

PAUL S. MINEAR, *Images of the Church in the New Testament*. Philadelphia: Westminster Press, 1960.

A thorough-going listing and analysis of ninety-six images of the Church.

PAUL S. MINEAR, *Jesus and His People*. New York: Association Press, 1956.

An excellent brief introduction to the New Testament Church.

J. ROBERT NELSON, *The Realm of Redemption*. Greenwich: Seabury Press, 1951.

A scholarly summary of ecumenical thinking on the nature of the Church.

H. RICHARD NIEBUHR and DANIEL DAY WILLIAMS, eds., *The Ministry in Historical Perspectives*. New York: Harper & Bros., 1956.

By outstanding scholars on the development of the ministry from the New Testament to today.

H. RICHARD NIEBUHR, *The Purpose of the Church and Its Ministry*. New York: Harper & Bros., 1956.

An original presentation of the way we should think of the Church and its ministry today.

RUTH ROUSE and STEPHEN CHARLES NEILL, eds., *A History of the Ecumenical Movement, 1517-1948*. London: S.P.C.K., 1954.

The one essential volume on the movement toward Church unity, written by the world's experts.

JAMES D. SMART, *The Rebirth of Ministry*. Philadelphia: Westminster Press, 1959.

Church and ministry seen from a perspective which includes education.

CLAUDE WELCH, *The Reality of the Church*. New York: Charles Scribner's Sons, 1958.

A study of the nature of the Church in the light of the incarnation.

E. R. WICKHAM, *Church and People in an Industrial City*. London: Lutterworth Press, 1957.

What happened in Sheffield, England, tells us a great deal about the Church's responsibility in the world.

ON EDUCATION

HORACE BUSHNELL, *Christian Nurture*. New Haven: Yale University Press, new ed., 1947.

After one hundred years, this new edition speaks to the current situation.

IRIS V. CULLY, *The Dynamics of Christian Education*. Philadelphia: Westminster Press, 1958.

Especially valuable for its analysis of the Biblical message and its dynamic use within the Church.

WESNER FALLAW, *Church Education for Tomorrow*. Philadelphia: Westminster Press, 1960.

An exciting book with radical suggestions concerning the teaching ministry within the Church.

NATHANIEL F. FORSYTH, ed., *The Minister and Christian Nurture*. Nashville: Abingdon Press, 1957.

Useful for its treatment of the teaching ministry and the significance of the Bible.

HOWARD GRIMES, *The Church Redemptive*. Nashville: Abingdon Press, 1958.

Theologically and educationally sound, this book is of the greatest importance in thinking through the Church's educational task.

REUEL L. HOWE, *Man's Need and God's Action*. Greenwich: Seabury Press, 1953.

This book has become almost a classic on the significance of relationships in Christian education.

CHARLES D. KEAN, *The Christian Gospel and the Parish Church*. Greenwich: Seabury Press, 1953.

An exciting attempt to discover the true nature of the Church and its educational functions on the parish level.

SARA LITTLE, *The Role of the Bible in Contemporary Christian Education*. Richmond, Va.: John Knox Press, 1961.

An acute interpretation of the theological bases of Christian education theory.

RANDOLPH C. MILLER, *The Clue to Christian Education*. New York: Charles Scribner's Sons, 1950; *Biblical Theology and Christian Education*. New York: Charles Scribner's Sons, 1956; *Education for Christian Living*, Englewood Cliffs, N. J.: Prentice-Hall, 1956.

W. ROY NIBLETT, *Christian Education in a Secular Society*. New York: Oxford University Press, 1960.

The latest report on the philosophy of religious instruction in the English schools, with suggestions on what needs to be done.

IAN T. RAMSEY, *Religious Language*. London: SCM Press, 1957.

An exciting new approach to the use of words for religious purposes; profound but not too difficult.

MARJORIE REEVES, *Growing Up in a Modern Society*. London: University of London Press, 1952.

Her insights into the nature of community can be applied to schools, homes, and churches; a significant book on Christian communication.

Religious Education, 545 W. 111th St., New York 25, N. Y.

A bi-monthly journal featuring Protestant, Catholic, and Jewish writers on most aspects of religious education.

GERARD S. SLOYAN, ed., *Shaping the Religious Message*. New York: Macmillan Co., 1958.

Important for many reasons as an example of the best Roman Catholic thought. See F. H. Drinkwater's chapter on religious language.

ERNEST W. SOUTHCOTT, *The Parish Comes Alive*. New York: Morehouse-Barlow Co., 1956.

The exciting story of the discovery of the nature of the Church within a parish and its homes.

MARVIN J. TAYLOR, ed., *Religious Education*. Nashville: Abingdon Press, 1960.

A cross-section of current thinking.

PAUL H. VIETH, *The Church School*. Philadelphia: Christian Education Press, 1957.

The best book on organization and administration of Christian education with a theological perspective.

BIBLICAL REFERENCES

INDEX

(The more important items are in *italics*)